SWIMMING WITH CHAUCER

Also by the author

At the Edge
Ghostwise
Next Teller
The Storyteller at Fault
Suddenly They Heard Footsteps
Tales for an Unknown City

SWIMMING WITH CHAUCER

a storyteller's logbook

Dan Yashinsky

INSOMNIAC PRESS

Library and Archives Canada Cataloguing in Publication

Yashinsky, Dan, 1950-, author
Swimming with Chaucer / Dan Yashinsky.

ISBN 978-1-55483-109-8 (pbk.)

1. Yashinsky, Dan, 1950-. 2. Storytellers--Canada--
Biography. 3. Authors, Canadian (English)--20th century--
Biography. I. Title.

PS8597.A85Z53 2013   C813'.54   C2013-906511-3

The publisher gratefully acknowledges the support of the Canada Council, the
Ontario Arts Council, and the Department of Canadian Heritage through
the Canada Book Fund.

Printed and bound in Canada

Insomniac Press
520 Princess Avenue, London, Ontario, Canada, N6B 2B8
www.insomniacpress.com

Achebe, Chinua. *Anthills of the Savannah*. New York: Doubleday,
1988.

Armstrong, Karen. *A Short History of Myth*. Toronto: Random
House of Canada, 2006.

Baugh, Albert C., ed. *Chaucer's Major Poetry*. New York: Prentice
Hall, 1963.

Benjamin, Walter. *Illuminations*, trans. Harry Zohn. New York:
Schocken, 1969.

Bringhurst, Robert. *A Story As Sharp As a Knife: The Classical Haida
Mythtellers and Their World*. Vancouver: Douglas & McIntyre,
2011.

Bringhurst, Robert. Introduction to Alice Kane, *The Dreamer
Awakes* (ed. Sean Kane). Peterborough: Broadview, 1995.

Calvino, Italo. *Six Memos for the Next Millennium*. Cambridge: Har-
vard University Press, 1988.

Courlander, Harold and George Herzog. *The Cow-Tail Switch and
Other West African Stories*. New York: Macmillan, 2008.

Cruikshank, Julie. *Life Lived Like a Story*. Vancouver: University of
British Columbia Press, 1991.

De Angulo, Jaime. *Indian Tales*. San Francisco: City Lights Books,
2001.

Garner, Alan, *The Stone Book Quartet*. London: HarperCollins UK,
1983.

Homer. *Odyssey*, trans. Robert Fitzgerald. New York: Farrar, Straus
& Giroux, 1998.

Kane, Sean. *Wisdom of the Mythtellers*. Peterborough: Broadview
Press, 1998.

Plato. *The Collected Dialogues of Plato* trans. Edith Hamilton and
Huntingdon Cairns. Princeton: Princeton University Press,
1961.

Tolkien, J.R.R. *The Lord of the Rings*. New York: Houghton Mifflin
Harcourt, 1988.

And which of yow that bereth hym best of alle,
That is to seyn, that telleth in this caas
Tales of best sentence and moost solaas,
Shal have a soper at oure aller cost
Heere in this place, sittynge by this post,
Whan that we come agayn fro Caunterbury.

Chaucer, General Prologue, *Canterbury Tales*

Some of the pieces in *Swimming with Chaucer* appeared in the following magazines, journals, and newspapers: *Toronto Star*, *The Globe and Mail*, *National Post*, *paperplates: a magazine for fifty readers*, *Tale Trader*, *Today's Parent*, *Canadian Jewish News*, *The Jewish Standard*, and *The New Quarterly*.

Many thanks to the Ontario Arts Council for the 2009 Chalmers Arts Fellowship, which enabled me to work on this book.

To those who have shared this storyteller's house: Carol, Natty, Jacob, Palomba, Bernard, Larissa, Abby, Mary Anne, and much-missed Jack and Michelle.

TABLE OF CONTENTS

INTRODUCTION

Many years ago I memorized "The Miller's Tale." I was driving around southern Ontario on a storytelling tour and had a lot of kilometres to cover. I drove up and down concession roads on my way to gigs in rural libraries, reciting line after line of Middle English and trying not to get too lost. By the end of the tour, I'd banged six hundred lines of rhyming Chaucerian couplets into my head. This could be the most useful thing I've ever done in my life. Geoffrey and I have been pals ever since, and *The Canterbury Tales* – in particular, "The Miller's Tale" – has been my steadfast companion for more than thirty years. There are those who, for solace, turn to scripture. I turn to Middle English couplets when times are tough. Besides crisis intervention, having poetry in my head also helps with more mundane experiences; for example, I run lines while swimming laps or when I'm stuck in rush hour traffic. Being a professional storyteller, I also know a few hundred folk tales by heart, a quantity of jokes (the kind that, having heard them so often, make my sons roll their eyes, often simultaneously), and a fair number of family chronicles. This headful of stories, with Chaucer at the core, has been my main navigational compass in good times and bad.

This book is a collection of writings about what it's like to travel through the world as a storyteller. It is a kind of logbook, where distances, dangers, harbours, and homecomings are recorded in the form of stories. It also includes poems, essays, and seven of my father's letters as ways I've marked and measured my various journeys. Some of the pieces were published in Canadian and American newspapers, some in various, mostly obscure, journals and newsletters. The letters were sent to me by a worried, loving, sometimes critical father who lived a continent away from a son troubled by love, politics, identity, and poetry: all the things that grab you in your late teens and never really let go. They wound up in my logbook because, through his long-distance observation and wisdom, he was trying to help me find my bearings on those perilous and uncharted waters called the sixties. There are five stories placed throughout the book, connected – at least for me – to the themes and experiences of the sections they open and close. The stories – "First One Red," "Talking You In," "Stormfool's Cool Gig," "A Selkish Tale," and "Report of the Blue Djinn" — haven't been published before.

One of my favourite books is titled *Life Lived Like a Story*. It explores, mainly in their own words, the lives of three Yukon women elders. In the course of her friendship and research with one of those elders, the anthropologist and author Julie Cruikshank asked Angela Sidney what it meant to her to be a traditional storykeeper. "Well," she answered, near the end of her rich and generous life, "I've tried to live my life right, just like a story."

In my case, I've tried to live my life right, just like I imagine a working storyteller can and should do in these strange and unprecedented times. Part of the book logs the ups and downs of trying to make a living as a freelance storyteller in the early years of the twenty-first century. But mainly the book is about the way storytelling has served as a rough guide and working philosophy for everyday life: in families, in the neighbourhood, in the civic and political realms. From daily routines to extreme adventures, life is tracked and distilled and noted through the stories we tell about it. Stories are waymarkers.

My Romanian grandmother used to begin her fairy tales: *Once something happened. If it hadn't happened, how could I tell you a story about it?* This seemed to make sense to her, but it left me puzzled. I used to wonder if things happened *because* stories would be made from them. I also wondered if we only knew something had happened *because* a story ended up being told about it. Despite all my questions, I did accept and even find reassuring the deeper truth of her droll paradox, which is that stories are born from the happened somethings of real life and imaginary life. In a mysterious way, her traditional opening set the scene well for her traditional stories. They were full of polymagical encounters between creatures of all kinds, and, just like in her real life as a war survivor and refugee, her wondertale beings had to cross difficult, sometimes impossible borders on their way to freedom, love, and sanctuary. My grandmother's opening reminds us that there's an unassailably intimate bond between the real and the imaginary worlds, and that these worlds not only run parallel to but also sometimes splash over and into each other. These borderlands and world crossings are where the best—or at least the most necessary—adventures begin. It is in these borderlands that time and space and truth and emotion can be refolded around each other to make the imaginary pattern we call a story. In the case of my grandmother, some of her stories were about the war and trying to survive bombs and fascists. Others were long Eastern European folk tales about flying horses, golden apples, and irresistible destinies. All of them were accounts of things that had weight and substance and power, in whatever world they happened to happen in.

This book logs my visits to and passages through a series of personal borderlands, where transformations originate but seldom end. The places, only some of which are found on maps, include Santa Barbara, California, in the sixties; the neonatal intensive care unit at Toronto's Hospital for Sick Children; a very rich and reclusive man's private estate, where a lucky freelance storyteller got the best job of his life; my living room; the attic and bedroom of a carpenter in Chaucer's England; a hardscrabble farm in rural Ontario; Tel Aviv and Ramallah; Lac Roddick in Quebec; a Maniwaki flea market; many cafés where I go to work and eavesdrop; my beloved neighbourhood of St. Clair West in Toronto; City Hall; three fictional bedrooms in the realm of the Blue Djinn; a beach in British Columbia; and a summer camp near Bolton, Ontario. In all of these places, real and imagined, many *somethings* happened. If they hadn't happened, how could I tell you these stories about them?

1ST STORY: FIRST ONE RED

This story is a tribute to Florence Turner and draws on a journal I read after her death. Florence, a teacher by profession, wound up raising her three daughters on a small southern Ontario farm. Her journal records years of struggle, with rare but well-chronicled flashes of joy. Her granddaughter Sharon Ward spoke the wise and compassionate words that helped Florence finally leave this world. I knew Florence through my marriage to her other granddaughter, Carol.

I wasn't much for farm life, but I loved my horse. My sister Vera hated the farm even more than I did, and she didn't even have a horse to ride on and pretend on. Not that either one of us was much good at pretending. That land was poor; dreams made a thin crop. Although, I wonder if it was the land or the times: the Great Depression they called it afterwards. We tried for wheat, oats, some potatoes, turnips.

Laundry, and more laundry. Always plenty of that.

And the plums came in well most years.

Vera read and I rode. Lindy was her horse to begin

with, but she didn't take care of her, so Father gave her to me. Vera just shrugged and closed her door and stopped talking to me for a few years. It was worse when she did speak, though, since most of it was mean talk, always snipping and clipping things down to size and even smaller, with all of her big, book-learned words. I felt like I could sit on a dime and dangle my feet.

My beautiful horse!

My beautiful husband! — and Vera never did get one for herself.

Ah — I meant to say: my beautiful red-haired daughters. My three beautiful girls. And to think they had beautiful girls, redheads again.

Red was in the quilt I made. My first quilt wasn't much, of course. At least it kept Gwen warm. Then she chewed the corner to a nub, and it was getting tatty, so I remembered my grandmother's trick and used the first quilt as stuffing for the second. The second was not bad at all. I used ten times more red patches and thread, and followed a diamond pattern I remembered from growing up. Even William noticed, and he wasn't the man to notice much.

That quilt, the second, even redder one, went to Sally. But by the time Edna came, didn't I put it away in the chest in the attic?

I made a third quilt.

Did I make a third quilt?

All red?

No, I could not possibly have made a third quilt — at least not one so bright and ruby-glowing as the one I see now, so huge, shimmering like a jewel, and stretching out to keep them all warm, poor girls. But I did not make the third quilt. No. It would have been too much red.

Who can I ask?

Problem with being so —

Stop being maudlin, Grace!

My mother's voice.

I'm Grace, I whispered into Lindy's white ear when Father gave her to me. You belong to me now. You're not Vera's pony. You are the one and only horse of Grace, from Milton, Ontario, third concession, the farm with the perfect barn.

My father built the best barn in the county, but I knew I wasn't ever allowed to say so. It was already built when I came along, but Vera always used to say that she'd handed Father the nails as he was building it. Galvanized nails, she'd say. His favourite nails, she'd say.

Lindy: my horse. Mine.

No, my husband was not beautiful. What he was, was quiet. Always working, then ill for so long. But whenever he held the girls, nobody could deny that he had a tender look in his eye, which was beautiful to see in a man.

I'm coming in through the kitchen carrying more laundry, and I see him sitting at the kitchen table, and there he has Gwen perched right in front of him, trying to grab his nose. He leans her back and then tilts her forward and on and on, and the glee that was in that little baby! Fresh, like the clean smell of the clothes. And William barely noticing me walking in, he was so taken by the game. But when he glanced over, oh, the gentle, loving look in his eyes. Which made me glad I was his wife, even if it meant farming.

I hurry by so he doesn't see me so close to tears.

Take a brace.

Mother's voice, or Father's?

One toot and you're oot.

That's Father, of course.

That night I wrote in my diary:

Four big loads of laundry today. Still hot, but I think a big rain's coming soon. The threshers should come on Saturday. Gwen can now say her name, but it sounds rather like "gin," to the amusement of Reverend McKnight.

Grandma, Grandma.

That's the voice of my sensible granddaughter.

Grandma, I'm never sure if you can hear me.

Of course, I can. I just don't remember your name. I know you are beautiful and have red hair like my Gwen, and Sally, and Edna, but I've lost all the other names. William's still here. His name.

Grandma, she says, we'll be fine.

We? My husband? Vera? My beautiful daughters? No, they can't be dead; they're much too young.

Gwen, of course, married a good man. Mind you, he gave as good as he got. He was the Mountie, so tall and handsome. Dashing. And he loved horses, too, and I told him about Lindy being named after Charles Lindbergh, even though she was a mare. He liked the land as much as I didn't. Of course, he only knew farming from those summer visits to his grandfather down by Lobo. It's different when you depend on it for everything, and have to count the eggs, and add everything up so carefully, and you're always scared there won't be enough.

When they were courting, I remembered the legend about that ghost around Rockton in 1934. They said that the ghost seemed to be especially fond of startling canoodling couples and lonely ladies. I told the girls the story when they were older and we'd moved away from the vicinity. They always asked me if it was true, and I always laughed. Then when Gwen was a beautiful young woman and she and her Mountie started dating, I reminded her of the ghost story and told her to be careful on country roads at night. That made her laugh.

Years later, I liked driving with them down from Ottawa, dipping down and swooping over those hills on Highway 7. William didn't like it much, but I've always enjoyed a fast ride in a car. One time we reached the outskirts of Toronto on our way back to Galt, William and me in the back, Gwen's husband driving, and we came to a green light, then another, then another. And he said, See, if this keeps up, we'll get right through the city without having to stop. And I piped up from the back seat, Yes, Sam — ah, I remember his name is Sam! — but what happens if you hit the first one red?

They laughed up in the front seat, Gwen's crystal laugh so lovely, just like when she was little and running around cracking silly jokes and rocking back and forth on the kitchen table with William just in from the barn and eager to play with his beautiful daughter.

Imagine all those cars, backed up forever, the lights red and red and more red, quite a fix that would be.

I glance over and sure enough William's eyes have his gentle look, hearing Gwen's laugh. He's ailing so badly by now, can hardly catch his breath in the back of the car. Can't let himself laugh because it would start him coughing. My quiet husband. I almost giggle at my own wit but don't.

I can't breathe myself.

I can't breathe.

Grandma.

Who's she talking to?

You can go now, Grandma. I love you, and it's okay to go now.

Ah — that is my granddaughter's voice. She's beautiful and just as red-headed as Gwen. She's the one who loves to ride horses. She's the sensible one who's always here talking to the doctors. They aren't country doctors anymore, not here, always hurrying past us. I've never liked my doctors too ornamental. How did my granddaughter learn to be so patient with a ninety-five-year-old? Patience was never a virtue that ran in the family. There she is every day next to my bed made of —

Grace!

Vera's voice.

Grace, you were about to say "bed made of clouds." There's no such thing!

Please, Vera, peace. It's time for peace, sister. Or I'll go ride Lindy, who used to be yours, but you didn't take care of her.

I won't take any more pills. I will keep my mouth closed from now on.

Grandma.

My granddaughter hasn't left.

She's talking to me; she's talking so gently I turn my face towards her and listen and almost smile.

Grandma, it's time for you to go to Mama and Papa, and teach your pony some manners so she doesn't throw us off when we get there.

Lindy's strong back's between my young legs, and I'm calling back to my red-headed granddaughter over my shoulder, galloping through the back field, calling back fierce and seven years old, my William made the best Christmas fudge in the county, and I know I shouldn't brag, but it's true, and it isn't so terribly bad to go canoodling, but watch out for ghosts, and did you know that your old quilts just go on keeping your loved ones warm as the innards of your new quilts, and get off the land if you can because it is such hard work and it broke my beautiful husband, but he did love to rock each one of you, your red hair in a mad rush, back and forth on the kitchen table, so gleeful and wild!

And Lindy's turning into a bright red quilt lifting up, and I gallop and I gallop and I....

IN THE STORYTELLER'S HOUSE

The pieces in this section chronicle everyday life from a storytelling perspective. It begins with seven letters my father wrote to me in my teens while I was living a continent away and in sore need – though I didn't often admit it – of his loving counsel.

YOURS FOR BIG MAMAS

I'm a packrat. Every postcard and letter I've ever received is crammed into a dozen dusty boxes in my closet. When I was sixteen, my parents moved from California to Toronto. I stayed in Santa Barbara for university, ocean, mountains, and the sixties. As I stumbled through my late teens, teeming with melancholy, heartbreak, and bad verse, my father wrote dozens of letters to his distant son. These are seven of his letters.

October 3, 1968
Dear Happy-idiot,

Your letter was a source of both satisfaction and distress. I'm happy that you seem to be enjoying the fruits of California, both flora and fauna; and that is as it should be. But this shit about turning in draft cards and taking an active part in the Resistance Movement TURNS ME OFF. Why? You are trying to make an absolute value of your idealism in a completely relative world. Cynicism? Yeah, but of a very practical nature. I believe in thinking right and acting right within the limits of personal freedom; if one is to suffer some kind of physical pain, for example, a bust on the head for expressing an opinion, it's bad enough. But when, for expressing an opinion (and that is what you are doing when you resist the draft), one runs the risk of losing one's personal freedom, while the very persons to whom your idealism is dedicated show only disdain and ignorance of what you are trying to do, it represents nothing more than the highest folly. You promised not to act before the year is over; I expect you to stick to your promise! And what is more, I would want you to wait until you have finished your undergraduate work, but that's another argument.

Part of my philosophy in bringing you up has been a rather negative philosophy, based on a pessimistic view of humankind and its future. Oh, it's not a black kind of pessimism that depresses one constantly, but of a nature that lets one appreciate all of the possibilities of the present world situation. Where did I start? Yes, my philosophy of child upbringing. As you know, I have been "permissive," with an attitude that made me want to see you get as much out of just everyday living as was possible within the context of our – perhaps bourgeois – ethical outlook. But I have always wanted you to "enjoy life" (I don't know how else to put it) and to have as many pleasurable experiences from living as is possible. That's why I have always been so strong on travelling, etc. I used to have a horrible thought from time to time: What if my kid didn't live long enough to experience sex? How his life would have been lacking! Do you get the idea? Well, you're still not halfway there when it comes to filling up a life with experiences that make it worth living. And you want to ruin your chances already? Goddamit, be idealistic, but temper your idealism with a little practical sense. The draft is the law; if you can't change it by legal means, and you can't live with it either, then split: Live in a country whose laws you can stomach. The U.S. is going "right" at such a fantastic rate that the only title your idealism can earn is "anarchy."

One other argument (a below-the-belter) is that you never act in a vacuum: Your actions have an effect on those who love you. Can you imagine the pain of Grampa's last years knowing that his grandson is in prison? I'm not even going to talk about me, but what about your mother? Would part of your reluctance to accept my advice about waiting be a reaction to how your peers would treat your decision? This is a question that you must honestly ask yourself; for your actions should not depend in any sense on how you think they will be received by "the boys." I could go on and on offering different arguments, but I think that I have broached most of them in the past. Anyway, I refuse to "understand" any move on your part that risks prison for not cooperating with the draft. NOOOOOOOO. Don't do it. Channel your idealism in more constructive directions as you have been doing all along. You have never hesitated to involve yourself in worthwhile programs — civil rights, Vietnam, etc. — and I have been damn proud of you for your convictions and for your willingness to sacrifice yourself for them. I just draw that line at giving up personal liberty; it's a hundred times more horrible than you can imagine. And it accomplishes nothing; you wind up being grist for a mill that feeds the hate of the ignorant masses. Join the Peace Corps, run away to sea, go live in Cuba, in Israel, but don't risk your whole life for a gesture that will likely be completely futile. And don't deceive yourself with regard to the effects of draft resistance; you could get a sentence of three months or thirty years depending on the tenor of the times and whether or not some gouty, old judge had a good time with his *petite amie* the night before court.

That's enough rapping for the moment; I haven't written a letter as long and as confused as this one in my life. I hope that I have conveyed enough of something (I don't know what it would be) to dissuade you from a rash act, which you might regret for the rest of your life.

We'll probably be talking to you Sunday, so I won't add any of the social amenities. We are all well, working hard and enjoying it. Love, Dad

October 29, 1968
Dear Dan'l,

on days like this
i wipe my ass
very clean!

Your last letter – except for the haiku – turned me off. Very egocentric! It seems to me that you are in a "constant-concern-for-myself bag." "I am blue and why I am blue," "ego-games," "You and the local draft board and Myself are all starting to know me by my actions." You are really very full of yourself, to the extent where your act of resistance becomes a very phony thing. (Your rationalization of the penalties is very significant with this regard.) In any case, you aren't defining "yourself" by taking a moral stand on this particular issue; you have been defining yourself through *all* of your actions up to this point, and most of them have been very worthy actions which have made me proud of you. It seems as tho' your desire to martyrize yourself stems from a need to assert your ego in a very dramatic way. It reflects an almost middle-class-ego defense mechanism. In any case, think on it and don't do anything rash until you see me. You promised! Besides which (last comment) you take a great deal of pleasure in having mastered your fear of prison (ego again), but how can you master your fear of something about which you know nothing? (I think I mentioned this before.) In any case, fear is a healthy human mechanism, one designed to protect us from harm directed toward us by others as well as from harm we might do ourselves.

(next day) How are you? I am fine! How is the weather? It is nice here! See the dog run! etc. I saw a snowflake today, portent of things to come. The trees are all standing around kind of bare-ass, but there is a fly buzzing around my window, so I guess winter is not here yet. We gave you the big news from last week, Frieda's visit. We were surprised out of our knee-bones when she called, but it was a genuine pleasure to see a familiar face. I enjoyed myself with the baby; he's a happy, bright little kid. He removed a door bumper from the study door in about five minutes, and it took me a half an hour to put it back. Either he is some kind of genius or I am very stupid (take your pick).

Things are going well at our respective universities. There is an enormous amount of work, but I think that the work has advantages. We don't miss – at least in a pathological way – you or our friends too much. Stendhal said, *"Le bonheur est dans le travail"*; he wasn't far wrong. In any case, it is very stimulating to teach such a variety of things; this week, for example, I am teaching Racine's *Phèdre*, poems by du Bellay and Ronsard, Marivaux's *Le Jeu de l'amour et du hasard* (this last one, downtown), plus phonetics. We don't go out much except for official bashes (I still haven't gone to a Canadian movie house), but we don't do that either.

Give our regards to all of our friends. How is

Geneviève? Tell her hello for us. Love, Dad

P.S. Don't get yourself in a hassle with Barb's parents; she would be the one to suffer the consequences.

February 9, 1970
Dear Dan'l,

Just a few words to add to our telephone conversation of last night. Number one: Get rid of your guilt thing about Papa's money and the truck! There's no point in rationalizing about it, i.e., a lesson, an experience to learn from, etc. The main thing is that you can't change the past, so you say "I fucked up" and forget it.

Number two: You want to come and spend the spring quarter in Toronto? Great, nothing would make me happier as long as it is for the right reasons. I'd love to have your ugly face around for a while and even for as long as you want. What I don't like is the world-weary attitude that one assumes at your age in saying that there is nothing worth learning, no point in going to school, nothing is worth working for; you know all the clichés as well as I do. I would be in favour of your dropping out after a B.A.; a year or two in the real world will convince you more than anything I can say about the necessity of preparing yourself for "something," and give you the incentive to expand your education in an area that you would find rewarding materially and spiritually.

I can see you either wincing or sneering at the term

"real world." I use the term advisedly. The life you are leading now doesn't reflect the kind of life you will have outside of your present artificial environment. Don't misunderstand; the value of your present environment lies in its very artificiality. You have the singular opportunity of being able to learn and to enjoy a great measure of freedom at the same time. You are responsible only to yourself. Life ain't like that.

I hate sermonizing, but you just don't seem to appreciate the value of your situation, and through your lack of appreciation, you are letting the opportunity of your life slip through your fingers. Anyhow, we'll have some conversations about all this when I see you at the spring break (I am very impatient to see you).

Number three: Phone conversations are shitty. When I asked you if you were balling your chick, it wasn't a serious query. The fact that you answered in a serious way made me somewhat ashamed of the question. Of course that's not what is important. Even explaining what I mean is stupid. Do I make myself clear? (If I were certain of making myself clear, I wouldn't ask, would I?)

Hang loose, babe! Do you know that I haven't had my hair cut since I last saw you? Talk about shaggy papas! I think I'll let it grow till you come home. I'll shock the shit out of you at the airport. Love, Poppa

Undated, 1970
Dear Dan'l,

Looks as tho' we are going to be hit by another postal strike, so I'm writing to beat the deadline and to return the enclosed cheques to you. We received your mask letter today. I'm still trying to figure out the importance of running around with a greased-up face. Most people wear masks all the time anyway; it's rare that one sees a bare face. At first thought, it seems like an attention-getting device – I haven't gotten past the first thought yet. Come to think of it, the kiddies do indulge in the "mystery of ritual" from time to time, only it used to be called Halloween. By the way, it must be nice to be able to drop forty clams with no sweat, more than most average families can save in a month. How does it feel to be a playboy? All right, now that I've gotten all the nastiness out, I'll turn to pleasanter things.

You must have gotten the impression from our phone talks that the house is working out fine. So far, it looks like the best move, figuratively and literally, we could have made. Especially from Mom's point of view. She is undergoing a transformation – lots happier, more positive, interested in her appearance, losing weight, etc. We have a richer social life with people just dropping in because we are so centrally located. I'm enjoying it as well. In fact, I have somewhat the same feeling I had when we first went to Calif – a feeling of living more intensely and getting more out of just being around.

The neighbourhood is full of "types", many students, lots of pretty girls, old coots, hags, dogs, cats, and squirrels. To say nothing of pigeons who coo and shit all over our roof. Mom and I have gotten in the habit of walking every evening, at least down to Yorkville, then back through residential streets with the old, old houses. Each house is a new kick; I have never been so aware of the individuality of houses – naturally, we always lived in plasturbia. Here, each house has character, and its character is distinct from its neighbour's even though they are only three to six feet apart. Our street is like a rabbit warren because most of the old "jugs" have nine or so rooms and many take in roomers – mostly students. And in the warm weather, like tonight, you can see bodies hanging from every window. Noise and light and movement all up and down the street.

I'm working like an s.o.b., trying to finish the thesis, working on our first-year language program, preparing the course I'm to teach this summer. It's a drag, man! There are so many things to do that would be more rewarding – like sitting on the UCen lawn wearing a mask (oops, that just slipped out). While I'm back in the real-life scene, I should tell you that Grampa is ailing. I don't think that he is terribly sick, but he is starting to have old-age problems like bad circulation, which lately has resulted in swelling of his leg. He was in the infirmary for a couple of days but is out now. We'll just have to wait and see how he does.

I had an urge to sit down and write you a description of incidents that occurred in just a normal day about a week back, just to give you an idea of what it is like living around here. It's a long story, and it's after midnight, but I'll give it a go.

I had walked down to the University one morning to see some people and decided afterward to walk down to Yonge and Dundas to Coles Bookstore, who were supposed to have some screen scenarios in French that I was contemplating for use in the course I'm organizing. Anyway, on the way back, it started to rain. I had my trusty bumbershoot in my briefcase. Whipped it out and continued my walk. Long way – about two miles. Saw a pretty young thing waiting to cross the street. Sidled up next to her. "Why don't you share my umbrella?" Demure smile – she says, "I like the rain." I say, walking with her protectively, "I do too." I continue, philosophizing. "But I prefer not to get soaked." Rewarded by an appreciative smile and the remark, "I like to be in the country when it rains." "Yes, but rain in the city has its charm as well – reflections in the streets, colourful umbrellas." *Und so weiter, und so weiter.* She walked with me for three blocks past the spot at which she wanted to turn, completely forgetting what she was about, and took leave smilingly and repeating, "This is beautiful, this is beautiful."

Later on, standing in front of the house when old Charlie comes over from across the street. First thing he says, "Guess how old I am." I'm embarrassed. "Couldn't possibly." He coaxes, "Come on now, guess how old I am." "Well" – very hesitantly – "more than sixty and less than seventy." He, cackling like a Model T with spark knock, "Damn near eighty and as strong as any bastard on the block." Next question was, "How much did you pay for the house?" And then, "How many people you got living there? I see two cars in the drive." Then, "What do you do for a living?" Finally, "What do you think of Trudeau?" The bastard is ruining Canada, according to old Charlie, and he recites a reworked version of the Twenty-Third Psalm to prove it: "He leadeth me to lie down in the poorhouse, etc...."

I'm too sleepy for the third vignette, which concerns an old, toothless lady. You saw her when we went to Webster's for dinner one night. A sorry old sight but, as it turns out, full of piss and vinegar. In fact, Sam, who owns the smoke shop around the corner, doesn't take his eyes off her when she's in the store. Seems she lifts everything in sight.

I could go on and on about the people whose acquaintance I've made in the few short weeks since we've been here. But another time. For now, I take leave— KEEP YOUR HEAD STRAIGHT OR I'M GOING TO SNATCH YOUR ASS BACK HERE! Love, Papa

April 22, 1971
Dear Dan'l,

You are right. All kinds of personal communication has suffered in our century, verbal as well as written. Mass media has destroyed the desire to think, and with the desire has gone the capability. But it is especially true of letter-writing. To read the correspondence of a great writer – Voltaire, Flaubert, *par ex* – is to appreciate the lack of the art today. Voltaire's correspondence, in particular, is fascinating reading. Nowhere does his wit and intelligence make itself more apparent; and, besides, he documents a vast period in French history and in the history of French "letters." Sadly, I am a product of the cultural desert which has been misnamed "education" in the U.S. I didn't learn to *think* until I was thirty-five. And I still have a way to go before I can catch up to you. You had the extremely good fortune to get out of the high-school system before it had permanently warped your mind. Besides, we tried to make you aware of things outside of the rigidly controlled system from the first days of your reading career. It's a mixed blessing. With awareness comes anguish. And knowledge serves more to illuminate our ignorance than anything else. In any case, a somewhat restless awareness has to be better than blissful ignorance.

I'm rambling.

Your sekshual problems sound pretty normal for your age. You seem to say – in most cases – that it is your partner who needs more than a casual relationship. I have a feeling that it is the other way around and that you have difficulty accepting sex on a casual level. Which is all right. Normal for your kind of upbringing. Besides, you are a sensitive individual, which is something innate rather than culturally inspired. Consequently, you have a need for a deeper relationship. Accepting sex as simply physical pleasure mixed with a warm feeling of camaraderie, of complicity, takes a certain maturity, which comes with age. I expect you'll get there in a couple of years. Of course, I may be interpreting your situation all wrong; only you can judge that. I think, too, that I perceive a note of "inadequacy" on your part in your letter: "But she wasn't quite, and I was a little too soon." Well, that's just the way most girls are; and if there is blame to be laid for "inadequacy," girls have to share it. It takes a lot of practice to be able to "pace" yourself with different girls. There are so many physical and psychological factors involved, and no two girls have them in the same ratio. Anyway, as you know, the foreplay is all important for a girl. I've always made it a practice not to enter that "garden of delights" until it was deliciously oozing all over whatever I had been using to stimulate it, be it hand or tongue. Once you get it to that point, you cunt miss. Of course, it all takes a little "psyching out" before and during. Finally, the most important thing is to have complete confidence in nature and in yourself – good self-image!

And thus comes to a close another chapter in the

sex manual of that eminent doctor, Mr. J. Yashinsky. Yours for happy fucking. Love, Poppa

P.S. I blushingly recommend a good shot of whisky before lovemaking; it relaxes tensions and makes for more "staying" power.

April 30, 1971
Dear Dan'l,

Eulogious letter arrived. Made me feel good. I agree with you completely on the results of your upbringing. In a very pragmatic way, the proof of the upbringing is in the living. And despite basic fears and apprehensions – which everyone experiences – you have proven yourself as an individual, lo these past three years. Remarkable, really, for you were very young to be set free. All of the decisions in the past regarding your freedom and your capacity to deal with it have been difficult, and finally came as a result of two things: one is the confidence in nature that you mention in your letter – I knew you had the same basic strength and confidence as I did; the other is a certain knowledge that nothing forms an intelligent being as much as experiences, the more the better. Don't think I didn't sweat, though – still do, but not as much– through all of your various forays into the world: Nissokone, France, Israel, California.

You would be surprised if you knew how many people ask my advice about child-raising simply because they admire you. As tho' the net product – you at twenty – were strictly the result of my efforts! Obviously not true. However, I am flattered when they ask. I settle back in my chair, stroke my beard, fix a wise smile on my lips, and perorate. I really only have a couple bits of advice: Never say NO without thinking, and love the shit out of the kid.

Trivia – My buddy Rob decided that we should take the boat over to his shop in order to put a slick coat of spray paint on it. But before I describe that odyssey, let me tell you about how I picked it up from the chap who sold it to me. I had to get a boat trailer because his trailer wasn't part of the deal. So I bombed down to the little yacht club right next to the beach which we visited last summer – you remember, water cold enough to freeze the balls on a brass monkey; I took the Volks down the ramp and put my trailer under boat. Winched boat on to trailer. Hopped back in Volks. Revved up motor. Let out clutch, and...nothing. It wouldn't budge. Poor little 1200 cc Volks couldn't pull that big Mama out of the wet. Chap I bought boat from – nice guy – backed his rig up to my Volks. Attached a chain from his trailer to my front axle. We flew up the ramp. Of course, the boat wasn't positioned properly on the trailer; everything had to be adjusted: rollers, axle, winch, etc. But the big Mama weighs about 1600 pounds, and in order to adjust things, a jack and blocks are necessary. Anyway, we trailed it on home. Snugged her up into the driveway, and there she sat, slightly askew, but okay. Back to Rob. He came over on T'day afternoon, and we trailed Mama over to his shop. Smart move. The shop has big hydraulic jacks, etc.; it took us from 4.00 to 8:00 that afternoon. But when we had finished, Mama was sitting proud and high, radiating white from her new coat of slick spray paint. She's back at the house now, and I'm working her over slow and easy, tightening up, touching up, letting her know that I care. My slip will be available on May 15. Ontario Place has got to be the pussiest place in the whole world to keep a boat. We shall see!

I don't have time right now to begin the tale of summer 1970. But I have been ruminating on it and will soon begin the first installment. Be patient.

Yours for big Mamas. Love, Pappa

July 9, 1971
Dear Dan'l,

I am stealing a few moments this a.m. (Friday) from my course preparation to answer your latest missive, which just arrived. Your letter has a little taste of sour grapes with regard to Eva, but if that kind of rationalization lets you live more happily with yourself, *tant mieux*. You're probably still taking yourself too seriously (that's a stupid cliché, but you know what I mean; we all take ourselves seriously). It's a question of degrees and situation. Anyway, I suffered at your age, so why shouldn't you?

Talk about hot-neck syndromes! You should see me haul ass preparing for my linguistics course. Just one small step ahead of my students. I have a large class, twenty-eight students. I'm exploring.

Went out on the beat (Freudian slip) – read: boat – with Rob and a couple of adventurous young women. He has a friend who has a sister, so we just went out like a big happy family. We had a nice time, drinking and swimming, buzzing around the lake. But when we got back to the house, Rob, who has been making it with his girl for a while, shot upstairs for the *coup de grâce*, while I stayed behind making a determined effort to achieve the same end. I won't say that I didn't enjoy it. My gal was young, beautifully put together, and willing – up to the crucial point. To make a long story uninteresting, I was shot down in flames. Little ego shards lying dully on the bed bespoke of my failure. I found out later that she is going steady and wants to be true to her boyfriend. However, I am undaunted, and have since rebuilt the shards.

I had a visit from Hannah last night. She hasn't changed much except that her breasts have gone from apples to melons. She came with another cute-ugly six-teen-year-old friend, and they started the old Hannah/Yolanda bit. Getting a big charge out of titil-lating the old man, secure in the knowledge that they are safe. Hannah wanted me to feed her drinks, which I refused to do (she really likes to "slosh"). But she was so insistent that I finally split a beer between them.

They arrived at about 11:00 and stayed till 1:00, talking trash all the time. "C'mon, Jack, just one drink. You can have my body for a drink." Hannah reeled off a string of dirty jokes that would have made a sailor blush. Anyway, I enjoyed observing and entering into the "play."

The neighbourhood is changing, as you will see when you come for your visit. A Scientology bunch has taken over the funeral home on the corner, and they are attracting a lot of Rochdale types. There is a constant turnover of girls in the various rooming houses, and I am astonished by the fact that most of them are lovely. Or is it me?

You can come when you want to. There are no restrictions or needs that have to bear on your decision as far as I am concerned. That's not quite true; of course I am anxious to see you again, but I consider my needs secondary to yours. In fact, (as you know) I am happiest about you when I know that you are doing that which makes you happiest.

So…back to the preparation and the ass-hauling. I will keep you informed about my various adventures… do the same. Love, Poppa

P.S. It's true that the trip to Calif was good for Mom and me. We have been getting along beautifully.

JEWS AND BEARS

I learned to be Jewish not by going to synagogue but by listening to my mother's and grandmother's stories.

The phone rings in the cottage: an unwelcome sound on a sweet summer day. I grouch my way up from a nap and stomp over to the big, cumbersome, cord-bound phone. The owner of the cottage, a very old friend of ours, doesn't do cordless anything up here. The harsh clangour of the phone can be heard down on the beach, but I'm the only one inside. That phone is tolling for me. But who could it be? Someone calling from work? Unlikely. Our nineteen-year-old son reporting a police raid on our Toronto home after an all-night beer bash in the backyard that a hundred wild guests crashed because word got out to every teenager in the city? Unlikely. I hope. My mother? Likeliest. I pick up the receiver and grumble a hello. It's my mother. Despite my telephonic phobias, we manage to have a surprisingly peaceable conversation — something about her not knowing where I'd put our dog's arthritis medicine – and, as we say goodbye, she makes me laugh. "Have you run into," says this Romanian Jewish survivor of the war, "any bears or anti-Semites?" I laugh, and admit that no, this summer, here on the bright shores of Lac Roddick, outside the village of Bouchette, Quebec, in the middle of the Gatineau Valley, there's been a distinct dearth of both bears and anti-Semites.

Her question was rooted in family history. A few summers ago, when my father was still well enough to make the trip, my parents had driven up to visit us. It was a highlight – as anybody who has had an attack of cabin fever would know – to drive up to Maniwaki to visit the Thursday morning flea market. It has fishing gear, miracle car wax, old tools, T-shirts with Che/Tupac/Elvis, French country and western cassettes, black velvet paintings, and fresh fruit. My mother and father had just bought some wild blueberries when another customer stepped up to the table. He ordered a basket of blueberries, but found the price a little high. The farm woman, probably tired from picking the damn things, wasn't in a mood to bargain. The man finally muttered, in his good Gatineau accent, "*Eh bien*, don't be a Jew!"

I doubt that he had ever met a Jew in his whole life. Call me naive, but I also doubt that his soul was deeply tainted by the foul corruption of bigotry. It was probably just a turn of phrase. But I have absolutely no doubt that in his worst nightmares he hadn't imagined

that one day he'd spout that ignorant expression standing next to a Jewish French professor who had survived
the Holocaust in Romania. My mother, all five feet
three of her, turned to this unfortunate citoyen and
chastised him in her impeccable French: *"Monsieur, vous
êtes raciste!* I am a Jew, and I was in the war. You are
wrong to speak in this way!"

This must rank as one of the great coincidences in
the sordid history of racism. What are the chances a
dumb comment is made unwittingly at the very elbow of
a member of the insulted race, and that said ambassador
of a disparaged people can summon – *a l'improviste* – such
eloquent, courtly fury to dispatch the perpetrator? The
man slunk away abashed, disappearing in the crowd but
immortalized in our family legends.

So that's why it made sense for her to ask about anti-
Semites. But what about the bears? A few years ago we
did see a bear on the mile-long dirt road that leads to the
cottage. Then we made the idiotic mistake of mentioning it to her. Never, my friends, never tell a mother
(Jewish or not, I suspect it works across all races and re-
ligions) you've seen a bear. The cottage is already, in her
imagination, a minefield of potential disasters. Poison
ivy, drowning, tornados, rabid foxes, snakebite, bees and
wasps, escaped prisoners, chainsaws: They start to sound
like a lakeside version of the plagues we name at
Passover. Now add bears. Ever since we told her, every
time we head north, she implores us to be careful about
the huge, ferocious, possibly anti-Semitic bears. She

probably pictures them popping off the flimsy roof of the cottage and scooping us up like so many soggy fries in a container of (at least kosher) poutine.

But behind the bears of her overactive imagination are other terrors, and these, unfortunately, she saw with her own eyes. She grew up as a girl in the war. She remembers hiding from the fascist police, the dreaded greenshirts who were as brutal as the German Gestapo, as they hunted down Jews. She remembers being bombed, first by the Allied planes returning from the oil fields of Ploiesti, then by the Nazis trying to destroy Bucharest before the Red Army arrived. She remembers rushing down a street looking for a doctor for her sick mother as a German fighter strafed her. She also remembers a Russian officer coming in the middle of the night for a billet. By the grace of God, the officer turned out to be Jewish. Her mother, raising a sixteen-year-old girl alone after her father was exiled by the fascists, called out, "Come, my darling, don't be afraid. He's one of our brothers. You will be safe." She has seen more violence than I can ever imagine, hidden from machine guns and the malice of her fellow citizens, struggled as a refugee in the New World, carried the weight of a troubled epoch on her slight shoulders. She can deal with anti-Semites in a Maniwaki flea market, and, if she ever met our bears (oops, I meant "bear"), I suspect my mother would walk out of the woods first.

Phone call over, it's time to swim over to the yellow

boat a half mile away. Yes, yes – with a flotation device
tied to my trunks.

Once Something Happened

For my mother, an elegy for a lost fairytale.

There's a story she heard once,
A golden tale, a shining tale,
And it began like all the stories
She heard when she was young:
"Once something happened –
If it hadn't happened,
There'd be no story left to tell."
And in this story a happy girl
Lived with her good mother and her strong father
In a warm house with many rooms,
And aunts baked and uncles teased,
And there was a maid and a white dog
And Easter eggs even though
They were Jewish.
And they lived in a beautiful city
In a prosperous country,
And people played an instrument with many strings
And ate roasted chestnuts in the cold season,
And spoke a language full of diminutives
And amusing proverbs
And one of those proverbs was:
"If you're born on a lucky day,

No harm can ever come your way."
Then she remembers the war begins and the story stops –
The father has to go away for seven years,
The aunts and uncles flee,
The mother worries about food and hiding places
And her own sick parents, who finally die,
And the dog runs away, and the maid disappears.
The house shrinks to a single room.
The city succumbs to bombs.
And her mother tongue tastes sour in the girl's mouth.
One day the war stops, but nobody ever tells her the rest of the story.
People get on boats and leave that country,
And she too goes to a new place,
Learns a new language, gets married, raises a child, works.
She grows older in that new land.
Now she knows she will never return.
She has never gone back to her first home –
She's afraid to travel alone,
And her husband is indifferent,
And her child is too busy.
She will never return, yet she has a great hunger
For news of that land where she grew up.
She'll ask even strangers, if they speak her language.
She'll ask them if they've ever heard of that old story.
She asks them if they can tell it to her,
That golden tale, that shining tale.

A REPLY TO JAMES

"What is your life?" I hate that sign. I bicycle past it every day on the way to the daycare. It exhorts the passersby from the wall of an out-of-the-way West Indian church at the corner of Arlington and Benson. They have it wrong, of course, and this gives me a twinge of satisfaction as I pedal by. The quote should say, according to the King James Version: *"For* what is your life?" It's just one word, but I do think that if you go public with our saintly wisdom, you should at least get the words right. The sign continues: "It is even a vapour, that appeareth for a little time, and then vanisheth away."

My son is strapped safely into his bicycle seat as we ride along (safely: when I remember to do up the buckles, which is about half the time). He is three years old and specializes in non sequiturs. As we pass a streetcar stop on St. Clair Avenue, he pipes up, "Lots of policemen!" I say, "What?" before I remember that six weeks before, he'd seen five police cars converge on the scene of an accident at that very spot. So his observations aren't so much *non* as lengthily spaced sequiturs. He seems to like his daycare. He gallops away to join his girlfriends after I drop him off. When I pick him up in the afternoon, I can always find him in one of the two enclosed spaces on the playground, under the slide or in the wooden cabin. He is cooking sand soup with Emily, Katherine, Tamara, Tiffany, and Rachel.

What I mind about the quote from James 4:14 is that it is so bloody obvious. It proclaims its cheap fact to the quiet Toronto side street with all the subtlety of a stripper showing up at a sedate birthday party. Life is a vapour. So what! I want to shout as I wheel past, my son balancing behind me on the bike. Him too, you bastards? Is he just a vapour on his way to vanishing? But of course I don't say a thing. James is right – undeniably, implacably, irrevocably right. My boy, his aging father, his mother, the daycare, the whole town – all, all does a little dust dance and disappears. There is nothing to say. So I ride a little faster, squeeze my little boy a little more tightly before going to work, and curse the complacency of churches that never change their billboards.

There are many routes to the daycare, but I always make the turn on to Arlington before I remember what lies ahead. In the afternoon, being more alert, I'm more careful in my choice of streets. But in the morning, not quite awake, the sign hits hard. As I go right on to Benson, I remember that I still haven't made out my will. Then I think – since it *is* true, after all, since we're all going to die one day (in fact, my heart's been giving the odd and uncomfortable thump lately, and I remind myself again that I really should make an appointment with my doctor) — I'd better let our son know that I won't be around forever.

But how absurd! comes the next thought. He's only three, too young to understand. As if there were an age when you do make sense of it. I'm forty and still haven't a clue. How would I even begin to explain? What do you say? My own father has never been very forthcoming on the topic of his own demise. Why should he be, you think, seeing as how it is a universal and hardly noteworthy fact of human life? But, no, if you never say the words, if you never lay claim to this particular inevitability, it seems to loom even more in the minds of those who will one day mourn you.

I tried to force the issue once when I was about ten years old. My father chainsmoked unfiltered Camels, and I spent the day leaking tears until, in late afternoon, I burst out, sobs and all, "You smoke too much!" He was sitting next to me on the couch, and, with a grand gesture, he took the pack from his shirt and flung it across the room. "I'll never smoke again!" he said, as the white cigarettes scattered over the floor. He did, of course, about a week later; but for that one moment we felt strong and close and united in our vanquishing of death. We had summoned and challenged and uttered the name of the Lord of Oblivion.

Perhaps it should be done like an initiation into the Mysteries. Fathers should tell their sons at the proper age and with due solemnity. *Boychik*, they should say, I've got news for you. One day you'll call for me and I'll be gone. The house'll be empty. It's called death. It comes to every living creature. It is not good and it is not bad. Having you, having children, seems to help. That's the way it is. And by the way, here's what I want you to do with my body.

Fathers should always give full instructions as to the disposition of their remains (I almost said "leftovers"). Give me a funeral with all the trimmings; or bury a pot with my ashes in the back garden; or get six handsome gamblers to carry my coffin, and so on. You see what I'm getting at.

Anything but the stark self-importance of James, so full of his deathly news. Life is a vapour. Yah, yah — you're all just stacks of ambulatory carbon.... You too will dissolve, disintegrate, be recycled through the table of elements. Yah, yah. Yes, James, you create your effect, you make your sensation. Like a very cold wind, your words halt the business of life, the hearse rolls by, the cop wearing white gloves stops the traffic, we all doff our caps, we all think, for one mortal moment, of the momentary mortality of our lives. This world, as Chaucer says, is full tikel, sikerly. But then the cashier rings in the bill, the mail's shoved through the slot, the afternoon lovers slide their hands on slippery skin, the daycare kids gather for their snack. Reckless, heedless, thoughtless creatures that we are, we're more entranced by the evanescent vapours, the "tikel"-like quality of life, than by your stern sputterings on the church wall.

Before that particular statement, you say, with your typical humour, "Whereas ye know not what shall be on the morrow." And before that: "Go to now, ye that say, Today or tomorrow we will go into such a city and continue there a year, and buy and sell, and get gain: Whereas ye know not...."

Oh come on. Get over yourself. Nobody can live by death alone. Are we supposed *not* to enter the city, not to plan our lives, not to buy the house (yea, even unto the second mortgage), or load our children on to the backs of bicycles, or pedal into our various and vulnerable futures? Just because our skeletons and all they carry are only temporarily animate, does that mean we should stretch ourselves out daily on our graves-to-be and bemoan the heartbreaking boniness of our too-brief being?

On the other hand. On the other hand, which is your hand, James, the final hand to be dealt, the losing hand that always wins in the end. On *that* hand, James, what do I tell my son? That one day I'll be scraped from the face of the earth like the pebbles I dump from his running shoes each day when I bring him home? What do you say?

But how absurd, I think again, leaning into the curve on to Benson. I have no intention of pegging out just yet. Vapour be damned. I'm not ready to vanisheth. Surely it can't be time to worry about how I'll take my departure (but I really must book that doctor's appointment, and call a lawyer – do I even know any? – about a will). I don't want to read the damn sign this early in the morning. As I coast downhill from St. Clair to the daycare, my boy clutches my back and squeals with terrified glee from the speed of it all: "Be careful, Daddy!"

For what is my life? *For* what is it?

SUNDAYS IN THE REAL WORLD

A few years ago we started a new custom in our house. It is known as Screenless Sunday, and, after a skeptical launch, we now observe it faithfully. Once a week we take a holiday from televisions, videos, computers, the web, iPhones, and even the lowly Game Boy. On Screenless Sunday every one of these marvels of modern communication is completely banished from our lives. For one whole day each week we're stuck — more or less willingly–in real life.

It all started because the dog was getting jealous of the TV. Mishigas (our aptly named Border Collie) would greet our two sons gleefully at the end of the day, only to watch them plunk down in front of the television, video, or PlayStation. Sensing she'd disappeared from their personal radar, the dog would trudge dispiritedly to her crate to brood on her unrequited licks. I knew exactly how she felt. I found that often when I was in the mood for contact, conversation, some modicum of human exchange, the boys would be sitting slackjawed and glazey-eyed in front of a screen. Even though they were only watching about an hour a day plus Saturday cartoons (a barbaric limit, according to them), I was still going around grumbling about it. That's when Screenless Sunday was born. I proposed to the family that at least once a week we'd have a time free of electronically generated images and sounds and voices. The attention we mustered on that one day would be, for better or for worse, spent entirely on living, breathing human beings (and a dog).

At first, of course, the kids thought I was completely crazy (mind you, they consider themselves deprived because we don't have cable). We took a vote. Both parents wanted to try it, both kids voted against it. According to the uneven citizen rights of family democracy, it was voted into law.

I have sometimes described our unusual custom to other parents and invariably got an amazed response. Everyone seems to like the idea of a day without screens, but most people tell me wistfully they doubt they could make it stick in their own homes. It's no wonder. The screens in our lives have proliferated like electronic loosestrife. Starting in our living rooms in the fifties, they've metastasized into every corner of every room of every house. My storytelling work takes me into lots of schools, and I sometimes do a survey of the children. How many of you, I'll ask in my most scientific polling style, have more than one TV in the house? How many have one in your own room? How many watch TV before school? How many of you watch during supper? In most classes, rich or poor, about 75% of all children answer yes to the above questions. In a suburban school, I once asked who thought he or she had the most televisions in their home. A grade eight boy mentioned that he had seven, no, eight if you counted the one in the bathroom.

Do the screens themselves do any harm? I've never worried too much about the content of TV shows – Ninja Turtles, Power Rangers, Batman, Xena: Warrior Princess, whatever (the boys' mother would vehemently disagree with this opinion). While I don't doubt that watching innumerable murders and seductive ads in their tender years isn't great for young minds, I figure that an hour a day of this vile stuff can't do anybody too much damage. It also happens to be true that both world wars of this century were fought by young people who'd never watched TV, let alone played a violent video game.

No, what worries me far more than the content is the way all of these screens have stolen the time of our lives. This daily mugging takes place every day in the supposed safety of our own homes. And not only do we not defend ourselves against the theft, we mostly hand over the goods willingly and without counting the damage. What most frightens me about our screenful lives is this constant erosion of time: time to talk, to be quiet, to fight, to rejoice; time spent without a sound-track of TV noise, or illuminated by screen light. We've created – or drifted into – a world where, surrounded by screens, our children are more familiar with broadcast voices than the voices of their neighbours.

Screenless Sunday has become our family's rear-guard, small-scale act of resistance. I should probably admit that Sundays chez nous are not always calm, peaceful, screamless experiences. Sometimes enforced reality brings out everybody's rougher edges. Turning off screens doesn't guarantee bliss or wisdom or brothers (or parents) acting like angels. In fact, there's often a distinct surge in the desire to visit friends' houses where our weird rules don't apply. But mostly we look forward to a once-a-week freedom from screens. For the kids, there seems to be lots more time during the day. Books get read, games get dragged off the shelf, my eldest gets to beat his father at crokinole, the youngest gets to surpass me at Scrabble. The dog enjoys especially long gallops through the ravine. For us parents, there is something very satisfying about not having to hear "I just have to beat this level!" or "Wait'll the *Simpsons* is over!" when it's time to do a chore or get out the door. The house, without any electronic visitors, is all ours for one day.

LIKE-MINDED

I'm looking for his underpants, and I've forgotten I'm already holding them. I holler when I discover my goof, and the six-year-old to whom they belong cracks up laughing at his old man.

Then he does an instant narrative replay of the scene. With all the urgency of a Buffalo *Eyewitness* newscast, he says, "So he's like..."–and proceeds to act out my part of his own eyes-to-the-ceiling, finger-twiddling-at-the-temple response to this latest example of grown-up idiocy. In the space of thirty seconds, he's created an extraordinary bit of storytelling. There has been a verbal zoom ("he's like"), a close-up on the main action (me looking for underpants, discovering them in my hand, yelling), a cutaway to his own reaction shot.

What I notice about these narrative "takes" – not quite stories, yet more than mere tableaux – is that they are cued by a strange use of the word *like*. Children say it all the time, of course, and it never fails to strike my ear and curiosity. As far as I can tell, this usage is a completely new twist on the English tongue. It certainly wasn't part of my argot as a kid growing up in Detroit in the fifties. The young man's grandfather, also from Detroit, deplores the ubiquitous *like*. Sloppy, ungrammatical, downright dumb-sounding, he rails, forgetting his own slang-rich working-class background. I, on the other hand, enjoy the way the six-year-old narrator gleefully masters a powerful new speech form.

It is so remarkable that I'm not even sure how to punctuate it. Should one deploy the mild, breath-based comma, as in "he's, like..."? That doesn't look or sound right, since the teller doesn't really pause in the flow of the telling and enactment of the scene. What does happen is that the storyteller leads us to the very edge of life-as-it's-happening, no past tense needed, no time even to say "he is," just "he's" and suddenly You Are There! But, as the very next word qualifies, you are not really there, only *like* being there, hearing about it in the teller's reportage rather than witnessing it first-hand. What *like* announces, in other words, is that what immediately follows is a likeness.

The young storyteller – and this is what strikes me as new and noteworthy – is impersonating a camera. His narrative moves to the jump-cut rhythms of camera and screen. He frames his dramatization with zooms, close-ups, cutaways. Word-mode seems to have fused with viewing-mode, and the camera's eye has infiltrated the teller's tongue. This means that the storyteller can spin an instant yarn, without detailing a sequence of events. He generates suspense through the intensity of his one-person enactment, not by the more conventional techniques of narrative. Rather than a controlled release of information, the six-year-old relays as much as he can as quickly as possible.

So let me suggest a new way to punctuate this new way of framing and telling stories. I'll use this high-floating ° to suggest the camera's wide-open eye as it begins to zoom in on the heart of the story. "He's ° like...!"

One probably can't prove the truth of a linguistic evolution when one is in the middle of it, but as a storyteller this theory makes sense to me. I think this may explain why our children today are so *like*-minded. If there's any truth to it, two other thoughts arise. The first is that our children are two generations deep into the age of television. They're growing up in a world where a good part of each day is spent watching images – likenesses, if you will – flicker across a screen. These pictures are beamed out of a variety of machines (television, video, computer, Game Boy) that occupy the very centres of the family's once-private space. Our intimate lives are conducted by TV light, our talk fits itself around TV voices, our sense of the world must inevitably reflect TV's non-stop flow of likeness.

Could it be that as the realm of the viewable expands without limit, the realm of the knowable is diminished? In a world where likeness rules, it becomes ever harder to perceive, remember, and narrate the truth of our everyday lives. The borders between daily life and broadcast image grow increasingly porous, and our children inhabit a world that is literally less solid, less real than the one we grew up in. The TV not only carries images into our lives, it drains the familiar and intimate out of them. And this is without mentioning videos, computers, and so on.

My second notion is that the children may be on to something. Could it be that what they're doing is subverting the immense, pervasive power of television by copying – and thus making more evident – its most subtle effect? Storytelling has always played a subversive role in society, mocking the powerful, imagining change, celebrating risk. If a certain degree of human experience leaks out of their lives through the many screens that surround them, perhaps our children's like-cadenced storytelling is a way they've found to resist this insidious damage. They've taken over the camera's reality-cramping power and use it to keep telling their own high-spirited and irrepressible stories.

I find it wonderful, and not really such a great surprise, that the ancient art of storytelling should help our children resist and subvert even such a soul-muffling machine as the TV. Perhaps they sense that they deserve more than the likenesses TV delivers, that they need to own their world more directly than the passive relationship to screen likenesses offers. So they've put to their own exuberant narrative use the very quality TV promotes, naming and trying to narrate their own deeply felt reality in the face of the ungrammatical but terribly real power of *like*.

FISHING AND CATCHING

We're rigged for muskie: a stout baitcaster, twenty-pound line, a wire leader, and a lure the size of a small torpedo. My son is casting into the boat basin at the foot of Bathurst Street, next to the derelict sugar silo and across from the Music Garden. We know these waters rarely float a sunfish, let alone the mighty muskellunge, but it's a good place to try out his new equipment. There are, according to Toronto fishing lore, some pike in the harbour, although we've never caught one or even had a follow. A friend at Al Flaherty's Outdoor Store tells us that you can catch them at the right time of day, the right season, the right water temperature, with the right lure at the right depth, and so on, and so on; but our hopes for a fish aren't particularly high. We're just happy to be down here, sipping lukewarm coffee, watching the lake bright with wind and late sunlight, companionably chatting about his day at high school and mine at work. We do a lot of fishing around Toronto, with meagre results. We often have to remind ourselves that the sport is called "fishing," not "catching."

Mostly we fish in a lake up in the Gatineau Valley. We have countless pictures of him standing proudly on the beach holding a surprised-looking bass for a photo op. Some we keep and cook, but most are returned to the dark waters of Lac Roddick. Around the Greater Toronto Area, truth to tell, we've caught more beauty than fish: a heron flying up the Credit River at dusk; a snapping turtle sunning itself at Eglinton Flats; the Don River sliding dark and mysterious before hitting the humiliating concrete ditch at its mouth; the sun going down behind the CN Tower as we stand on Leslie Street Spit trying for pike; the salmon leaping against the current on the Humber. My one notable success was landing a small trout at Heart Lake, in a conservation area surrounded by dreary subdivisions. My son, astonished, exclaimed, "You, of all people!" He knew that what I like best is driving the boat, cooking the occasional bass, and documenting his fishing victories.

The son I'm fishing with is our youngest child. It's amazing that he's here at all. When he was born he had an Apgar score of two. This is a measurement of vital signs, and six or seven is considered normal. He spent his first three weeks in the neonatal intensive care unit of Toronto's Hospital for Sick Children. Then, when he was four, he was diagnosed with Prader-Willi syndrome (PWS). It is a rare condition, the predominant feature of which is that the body cannot regulate appetite. People with PWS experience constant, maddening, insatiable hunger. Families living with this disability get used to locked fridges, careful measurement of food, and heartbreaking meltdowns when their children can't get at the food every misfiring nerve in their body is telling their brain they need.

He's a good fisherman. He has patience, tenacity, a formidable capacity to concentrate, and an uncanny ability to imagine where the fish may be lurking under the dark waters of the lake. Sometimes these qualities help him – and us – cope with PWS; sometimes we're swept away by it, discouraged and panic-stricken by crises none of us has the wisdom to resolve. But even on the bad days, days when we get the dreaded call from the vice-principal to say something's happened and could we come to the school immediately, even then we try to remember that he – like all teenagers with a disability – faces each day with more courage and heroism than many people muster in their whole lives. He knows, because we often tell the story, that his beginnings were precarious, and that his great-grandmother, nearing her own death, said, "He's here for a purpose." Once, as he was trying to get me to pick up the socks he was too lazy to reach for, I asked why I should do him that favour. "Because," he said, playing his heroic ace, "I chose to live." It didn't work, of course, but we both laughed. He also knows that his disability is an enormous, complex, daily challenge. It is difficult for a teenager with Prader-Willi syndrome to be in high school, to walk through a cafeteria filled with tempting food, to focus on academics when your body tells you to go secretly foraging for leftovers.

As all parents do, whether or not a child has a disability, we've learned to store up the good moments as ballast against the hard ones. We rejoice in the memory of his giving the opening speech at the Prader-Willi Syndrome Association conference, or performing a poem at an open mic, or using his exceptional sense of pattern to create a piece of beautiful gemstone jewellery or to win at Scrabble. We hold on to a sense of his immense generosity and sweetness as an antidote to the daily, demoralizing struggle with the syndrome's insidious effects on behaviour, rationality, and health. In other words, we keep fishing, even if we don't always catch what we're hoping for.

My favourite fishing story is about the first fish he ever caught. We were out in a rowboat near the shore of an island. His rod bent double, and I said, "You're caught on a log." He shook his head and whispered, "It's a fish." "It's a log," I affirmed with grown-up certitude. Then the line began to run out, and, after a memorable battle, my seven-year-old fisherman reeled in a two-pound smallmouth bass. I was wrong, as he's never tired of reminding me. I was wrong, and delighted to be so. I was wrong, but may I say in my own defense that it's sometimes hard for parents to tell the difference between a log and a fish?

So we're here at the harbour, ready for muskie (and he did catch one once, near Bancroft; I have the photo to prove it) but more than content to sip our now-cold coffees, watch the sunset, cast our lines (the strollers on the promenade give us wide berth, afraid his fearsome lure may snag their poodles), and remind each other of the Jewish proverb: It's better not to catch a big fish than not to catch a small fish.

WORDS OF MOUTH

I collect spoken words. Some people like to collect fishing lures, first editions, bird sightings, and sports cars. I hunt and gather the chance phrases I overhear on the street, in cafés, in my own kitchen. These words of mouth include family sayings, eavesdropped turns of phrase, proverbs, *bons mots* (and not-so-*bon* but still memorable *mots*), and every clever, impromptu phrase our sons have uttered over the years. Our youngest, age seven at the time, announced at Hanukah: "Dear family – I love you all very much so far." And, at the beginning of his science studies (grade one or two), he told me, with some alarm, "Dad, did you know Mom is a mammal?" More recently, when I asked him what it was like being raised by artists, he said, "Inexpensively eventful." Every son or daughter of a storyteller, poet, dancer, sculptor, actor would agree. His older brother, in grade five, spoke on behalf of children around the world when he said, "It's Play Day! We're not *supposed* to learn anything!" When he was three, his mother was trying to put him to sleep by telling him a boring story in a very monotonous voice. It was all about the animals in the barnyard going to sleep. "The piggies were getting sleepy … the cows were getting sleepy … the ponies were getting sleepy …." I gather she listed quite a number of animals, but it didn't work. He lifted his head excitedly and said, "Then suddenly, they heard footsteps!" So much for the soporific quality of her storytelling. His love of narrative suspense has carried over into his work as an actor and screenwriter.

Once, commenting on our sons' reluctance to move with alacrity when it came to doing chores, their mother coined the term *molassity* – now part of our oral lexicon. And when things aren't going so well chez nous, we recall what we overheard a young mother tell her fretful baby in a park in Paris: "*La vie est plein d'emmerdements.*" Life is full of little shittinesses. I revel in the way such words of mouth can strike my ear and stick in my memory. All of this daily, speakable feast is duly recorded in what my kids call my *Book of Quotes*, my collection of spoken words caught in flight.

My father was a fount of sayings, many of them inherited from his days selling used cars in Detroit. Even after he became a French professor at the University of Toronto, he had a way of bringing them forth when the occasion called for a wise or pointed comment. Our most famous one is: *Get out of the car!* My father had an African-American man working with him named Jerry Morgan. Mr. Morgan was always getting pulled over by the police, who would yell: "GET OUT OF THE CAR!" In *De*-troit we say "*po*-lice," and in my hometown in the fifties, Driving While Black was a risky activity – and still is, my friends tell me. Mr. Morgan, unabashed, took this phrase as his subversive life motto, applicable for both good times and bad, for singin' the blues and expressing elation. Now, via my father, it became part of our family's folklore. And from the southern Ontario side of the family comes the punchline, now a well-used saying: "You go ahead, Mary; I'll go back for the lantern." It comes from a story my in-laws tell about a nervous farmer who went with his wife to investigate a suspicious noise coming from their barn. At the last minute, our not-so-brave farmer turned back with that unforgettable phrase. We remember it in situations that call for courage, to remind ourselves how not to act.

Every family has its own mini-folk tradition, a private heritage of favourite sayings. Their humour and wisdom put a frame of imagination and meaning around our lives. Oral lore also connects us to the philosophy of our ancestors. An Italian friend told me that her grandmother used to say, "Grow old, red socks." It means that, at a certain age, you can wear anything you damn well please. Ever since I heard it, I've worn only purple socks. "You can't dance at two weddings with one *tuches*," my Yiddish-speaking friend Ros Cohen says, quoting her late father — a useful motto when it comes to making difficult choices. "What's for you won't go by you," a teacher once said at a workshop I was leading. The Zen quality of this has stayed with me. One of the most powerful things about traditional proverbs is that they can speak to us in different ways at different moments of our lives.

Sometimes I catch a phrase that would require a novel to explain. I overheard a young woman at one of my favourite cafés (not that I was eavesdropping, of course, but you probably don't want to sit next to me in public) say to her companion, "'Cause the reason was, my mom had another lover." My ears grew bigger and my mouth grew smaller, as I once heard a Danish storyteller say. "Your mother's got *another* lover?" I wanted to ask the woman. "Isn't one enough?" But I was discreet, and simply noted it in my journal.

We live in a time where voice, memory, and the ability to listen are all under threat. Kids retell television episodes more than anecdotes or folk tales heard from their grandparents. Maybe that's what I love so much about the oral culture that still survives. Even in the miniature form of sayings and proverbs, this marvellously expressive language needs a speaker, a listener, and its own timely moment. The love of the spoken word comes from societies where primetime means storytime. Speaking of which, a Ghanaian friend once told me, "The white man has the watches, but the black man has the time." We traded proverbs for a while. He liked this one from southern Ontario: "Never say 'Whoa!' in a mudhole." Then he told me one I remember every day: "If you want to walk fast, walk alone; if you want to walk far, walk with friends."

TALKING TO STRANGERS

We were strolling on a path by a lake when a man walked by. Our three-year-old son asked if we knew him, and we said, no, he was a stranger. Then he piped up: "We don't know any strangers, do we?" We had to agree that, no, we didn't know any strangers. But his question stayed with me. It's true that if you know someone, they're not a stranger anymore. But what about all of the people out there, unknown or not yet known, who may one day walk towards us on a path by a lake, or on a city street? How do we welcome – or at least acknowledge – those who will visit our world from the vast and mysterious Land of Strangers?

The old courtesies that taught us how to treat strangers have eroded. We no longer remember, for example, why it's important to share bread and salt with a stranger. In the old stories, and still in some places around the world, you offer a cup of tea before you even ask a stranger's name. The young don't even cover their mouths when they yawn, setting off the inevitable round of irresistible yawning in whatever company they're keeping. In our society, you can "like" a "friend" on a social media network; you can feel "linked in" to people you'll never meet; you can conduct all manner of business with people you never actually talk to. Who's a stranger if you can have a thousand "friends," each one "liking" you enough to send you the latest picture of their cat? Could it be that we have enough "friends" nowadays? Maybe it's time to start a movement to bring back strangers and the customs that help us welcome them?

When we put out an extra glass of wine for Elijah at the Passover dinner, I often think about the strangers in — or on the borders of — our lives. According to legend, Elijah never appears as a saint or a prophet bearing blessings. Instead, he shows up in the form of a beggar, a homeless vagabond, an impoverished stranger. That same son who was interested in strangers, age seven and a good listener to the stories he'd grown up with, walked by a panhandler in front of the drugstore on St. Clair Avenue West and asked, "Daddy, is that Elijah the Prophet?" "Could be," I told him as we put our usual quarter in the cup. At that year's Seder, we told the story about a man who wanted to see Elijah's face. He spent his childhood and youth staring at the extra goblet of wine, hoping that Elijah would appear, but it never happened. He complained to the rabbi, who told him there was a guaranteed way to see the face of Elijah. He was to go to the poorest family in the village and bring the best of food and the best of wine to their Passover celebration. Then, surely, Elijah would appear to him. He did as the rabbi suggested. It was magnificent, joyous, delicious, and completely unexpected. The poor family was thrilled and grateful. But still no Elijah. When he went back to the rabbi, disappointed yet again, the rabbi handed him a mirror, and said, "Look at the mirror. *You* were the face of Elijah the Prophet to that poor family."

I was walking down Spadina Road in Toronto one early evening when I was rudely accosted by two strangers. I had just come from the swimming pool at the Miles Nadal Jewish Community Centre and was clutching a little black swim bag. Coming towards me on the sidewalk were two big men, very drunk. I had a feeling there might be trouble, and there was. As I tried walking by, one of them stood in my way and said, "Get out of the way, you little Jew!"

This gave me a real dilemma. You see, I *am* a little Jew. I wasn't offended by the name, since it happened to be true. But I don't like being bullied. I learned this from my Romanian grandfather. When he was a little boy, the local bully taught him a bad word and told him he should say it to his mother. It was a set-up. The bully didn't mention that it was one of those words you should never, under any circumstances, say to your mother. His mother was shocked and appalled, and sent him on to his father. When he heard the bad word, his father slapped him. My five-year-old grandfather, ever vigilant to the finer points of social justice, pointed out that it was the bully who'd taught it to him, and he didn't even know it was one of

Those Words. Then his wise dad told him that the slap wasn't for him, it was for the bully. My grandpa ran outside and passed the slap on to the bully, and the kid never bothered him again. I'm not recommending this as a surefire way to deal with your neighbourhood bullies, but it worked for my grandfather.

Remembering this story, I knew I had to do something. I turned on the sidewalk and called out: "Hey!" They stopped and turned. I, little Jew that I am, walked up to them. I couldn't think of anything particularly heroic, noble, or edifying to say by way of repartee, so I just said: "Don't talk to strangers!" They mumbled, "Sorry, man …" and shuffled away .

A rabbi once asked his student how he would know that the light of dawn had come. The student answered, "When you can tell the difference between an olive tree and a walnut tree?" Good answer, but no. "When you can tell the difference between a dog and a goat?" No. Then the rabbi explained, "It is when you can look on the face of a stranger and see the face of your brother or sister. *That* is when you will know daylight has finally come."

Maybe what I should have told the two men on Spadina Road was: Don't talk to strangers, unless it is to offer some bread and salt, or invite them for a cup of tea. Then take a good look at their face, just to see if they look like your brother or sister.

2ND STORY
TALKING YOU IN

This piece grew out of my experience as a father with a son in the neonatal intensive care unit at Toronto's Hospital for Sick Children. It is a contemporary cantastoria *— a story set to music. I have performed it with composer/guitarist Brian Katz at festivals, conferences, and hospitals around the world. One of our most satisfying experiences was doing it a number of times for medical staff at the NICU at the Hospital for Sick Children. Many of them had just come off shift or were about to go to the ward. On the day's agenda taped to the wall of the drab classroom, "Talking You In" was listed between topics like "hypoglycemia" and "bereavement." Wherever we have performed the piece, we have heard extraordinary stories from the audience about their own experiences talking a loved one in or, just as significantly, talking them out. The Hospital for Sick Children published a booklet titled* It Was Midnight on the Ocean — The Neonatal Intensive Care Unit Book of Rhymes and Stories, *edited by Canadian storyteller and author Celia Barker Lottridge. This wonderful little book is now given to every family that comes to the NICU.*

They say that every human being
has a guardian spirit
an angel you could say –
and just before you're born your angel takes your soul
on a world tour.
You see your whole life-to-be,
your homes and your journeys,
your sanctuaries and your exiles,
the friends you'll make,
the lovers you'll take,
and everything that will happen
to you in your life.
And this world is so shocking and strange.
It's loud and spicy and smelly and way too bright
and unpredictable and full of emotion –
so different
from the celestial glory you're accustomed to
but also, in its own earthly way,
beautiful, desirable, irresistible.
Then, just before you're born,
your angel takes you to meet Worldmaker,
the One Who Made the World,
the host of the land where souls live before we're born
and return to when we die,
the Mystery of mysteries –
and you tell the story of what you've just seen,
the whole story of your life-to-be,
and Worldmaker listens with an infinite patience to
every detail

from beginning to end,
the whole story,
and when you're done
Worldmaker reaches out and touches you.
And at that moment,
you forget everything you've just told,
you forget your story.
The legend says that
this gift of forgetfulness
means that when we're born
we're able to see and feel and touch everything
as if for the first time.
And it also explains why
as we go through life
we sometimes feel
like we're catching a glimpse or hearing an echo
of a world we once knew very well.
The legend says that every human being carries the
mark
of Worldmaker's touch
on our upper lip
right underneath our nose.
For most of us the touch was light
and the mark shallow,
but this story is about someone
who has the divine dimple deeply etched
as if Worldmaker had to press extra hard
and give an extra dose of forgetfulness,
knowing how hard it would be

at the beginning
of his journey.

Once upon a time
in a room in Toronto General Hospital
a baby was born as sick as a baby could ever be.
We catch a glimpse before they rush him
to the examination table:
He is as white as paper,
eyes bruised shut,
a ghost baby
too weak for his mother to hold him.
We hear a doctor's voice explain:
"His condition is critical –
we've called the transfer team –
they will rush him
to the neonatal intensive care unit
of the Hospital for Sick Children."

We begin to slide
into the shock of catastrophe
where everything happens
in a rush and a reverie
too fast and too slow
at the same time.
We feel detached from the panic,
as if we're watching the movie
of our own emergency.

The doctors and nurses
huddle around him
taking his vital signs:
appearance
pulse
grimace
activity
respiration ....
We hear a doctor's voice explain:
"He has an
Apgar score of two –
six or seven is considered normal –
the baby's cord was wrapped around his foot –
there are subtle signs of genetic disorder –
we do not know why your child's so sick –
the specialists are on their way."

We sit holding hands,
and I say to my wife,
"He doesn't even have a name yet,"
and she whispers back,
"We can't let him die
without a name."
We quickly decide to name him
after a beloved grandfather,
my father, who'd died
not long before.
"Tell them our baby has a name now," she says,
and I hurry across the room

and say to the doctors and nurses,
"Our son has a name."
I say the name out loud.
Then louder –
And when I come back to her
we hold hands
and feel strangely comforted
now that our son has a good name,
and we murmur his new name again and again,
a small spell against oblivion.

But for this story
I'll use the nickname
we whispered late at night
imagining him
a small soul
a flickering flame
so far away
somewhere past the furthest stars
drifting on a dark and distant sea
seeking the way that leads to earth
his secret name
his midnight name:
Starchild

The nurses prepare a blood transfusion,
and I say to his mother,
"There's something I have to do,"
and walk towards the crib.

The nurses hand me a Polaroid,
and I think this is no time for photography,
then understand their wisdom —
it may be the only picture we have of him.
I lean over, reach in, touch the baby,
move the baby gently, gently,
a half a millimetre each way,
and gently sing the song I used to sing to his older
brother:
Dance to your daddy,
my little laddie.
Dance to your daddy,
my little boy.
You shall have a fishy
in your little dishy.
You shall have a fishy
when the boats come home.

I walk back and tell her what I've done,
and she, in bed, exhausted, says,
"Whatever happens next,
at least we've given him a good name,
and he's heard a song,
and he's danced with his daddy,"
and finally we can weep.

The transfer team begins to push the portable crib out
of the room –
I hurry alongside —

those nurses are fast!
Through the halls.
Down the elevators.
Through the tunnels
between the great hospitals.
Left, right, up another elevator.
We emerge in the Hospital for Sick Children
and hurry towards the NICU.
It is now the middle of the night.
I see the flashing green lights
hear the monitors'
Beep
Beep
Beep
Beep
Soundtrack of intensive care.
Get dizzy.
Fade to black.
Faint and fall upon the floor.

This became a legend
in the annals of the ward —
The night four babies arrived by helicopter,
twelve by frantic ambulance,
and one in a high-tech trundle buggy,
and in the very middle of the chaos
a father fainted,
fell, and slept peacefully
on the floor

while they calmly stepped around him
going about their business
saving lives.

And in my brief sleep
I have a dream —
I see a procession
carrying torches in the darkness,
singing joyful songs
and walking towards
a vast building filled with light
like an ocean liner on a midnight sea —
It is the Hospital for Sick Children —
So bewildering,
to hear such songs of joy
while I'm so worried about our own sick boy —
And as the people come closer
I see the face of the man
who leads them,
and it is my own beloved father
who'd died not long before
and behind him my grandparents
long gone
and teachers I'd loved
and a long line of ancestors,
and I understand that they have all
come from the land
where souls live before they're born
and return to when they die.

And I step into the procession
and walk towards the Hospital for Sick Children,
and even in my exhausted dreaming
I, too, join the jubilant singing.

And so we moved into the parents' lounge
just down the hall
from the NICU.
We were surprised
by the silence of the ward.
The mothers and fathers sit holding hands,
reluctant to ask about each other's children,
saying little about our own.
We wait for information from the passing nurses.
We wait for the doctors to bring
test results,
medical reports,
data from the monitors' non-stop beeps
that measure our children's troubled sleep.
Silently we keep our night-long vigils,
silently we pass our endless days,
silently we wait for the doctors to say
whose babies will go home that day,
whose are holding steady,
whose have begun to slip away.
We feel so overwhelmed
in the middle of this high-tech realm.
We lack a language.
We have no words.

We don't know what needs to be said
or how to name our nightmare dreads,
For some of us wish secretly for a merciful death,
others pray for a sudden cure,
and all of us fear
the lifelong pain
of a child born with a damaged brain.
If only there were a story to tell,
some piece of wisdom
to guide us through
the hopes and terrors of the NICU.
O Doctors,
you who can measure the faintest heartbeat
of the sickest baby,
can you measure the distance
a starchild must travel
to be born?

Late one night in the parents' lounge
another father said to me,
"It's like a silly rhyme I used to know
when I was a kid:
It was midnight on the ocean,
Not a streetcar was in sight....
That's how I feel —
like we're out in the middle of the ocean
and I don't know how to steer the boat."

One day my wife looked around and said:

"It's too damn quiet around here —
no one is singing lullabies
or talking to their babies.
If he lives, I don't want his first words to be 'beep beep beep' —
Go sing him a lullaby,
tell him about his big brother
and about your dad, who he's named after.
Tell him about the neighbourhood
and the house.
Tell him all your silly jokes
and every fairy tale in the world.
But hurry —
now's the time for some
emergency storytelling!"

And so I hurried down the hall,
entered the ward,
went to the crib,
leaned my forehead
against the Plexiglass,
and began:
How many miles to Babylon?
Three score miles and ten.
Can I get there by candlelight?
Yes, and back again.

Starchild, where are you?
Can you hear me?

Do you read me?
I know you're scared and lost
and reluctant to come here at all,
especially into this little body
stuck with needles and tubes and smelling of antiseptic.
But please don't go away.
We want you to stay –
we want you to walk in beauty one day.
Keep listening, Starchild –
Don't lose the signal, sweet boy,
and my voice will be a beacon you can navigate by.
If you keep listening,
I'll keep talking –
I'll talk you in
the way an air traffic controller speaks to a frightened passenger
who takes the controls if the pilot gets sick,
teaching them to fly and land a plane they've never flown before.
If you keep listening,
I'll keep talking –
I'll tell you the greatest stories in the world.
I'll build you a house of stories to keep the storms away.
Starchild, I'll make my stories
so suspenseful you'll never be able to leave
until you hear how the stories end,
and that will take a long, long time ....

Listen ….

Once there was an old man and an old woman,
and they had no children,
so one day the old woman made a Johnnycake —
a round little boy of fine, sweet dough —
and gave him two bright stars for eyes
and called him their "Starchild"
and put him in the oven to bake.
"Don't open the oven door,"
she told the old man.
But he opened the door and peeked inside,
and the Johnnycake jumped out and rolled away.
The old man said, "Come back here, Johnnycake!"
but the Johnnycake just kept going,
and as he rolled he sang this song:
Johnnycake ho!
Johnnycake hi!
No one can catch me
as I roll by!
And he outran the old man and came to the old woman,
and she said, "Where are you going, Johnnycake?"
and he said, "I outran the old man, and I can outrun
you, too!"
"No you can't!" she said,
and began to chase him —
but the Johnnycake ran even faster,
and as he ran he sang:
Johnnycake ho!
Johnnycake hi!

No one can catch me
as I roll by!
And he came to a cow and a horse and a goat,
who said, "Where are you going, Johnnycake?"
"I outran an old man and an old woman,
and I can outrun you too!"
"No, you can't!" they said,
and they began to chase him,
but they couldn't catch him,
and he ran on and on
out of the country into the city,
right down University Avenue
until he came to the Hospital for Sick Children,
and the doctors with their stethoscopes
and the nurses with their IV tubes
ran outside and said,
"Where are you going, Johnnycake?"
And he said, *"I've outrun an old man, an old woman, a cow, a*
horse, a goat,
and I can outrun you, too!"
And they shouted, "No you can't!"
and began to chase him down the street –
but he ran faster
and as he ran he sang,
Johnnycake ho!
Johnnycake hi!
No one can catch me
as I roll by!
And he rolled on and on

way past Babylon,
three score miles and ten
and a million times again.
Johnnycake ho!
Johnnycake hi!
rolling off the earth
into the sky.
See him fly,
breaking orbit
into space.
What a race
'til he was safe
and all alone
beyond the stars
so very far:
No one can catch me
as I roll by ...!

So what will happen next, Starchild?
How will the story end?
When the thread's been broken,
how will it mend?

Days passed and nights passed,
and we told him every story we knew
and then began to make them up.
We read him *The Jungle Book*
and *Just So Stories*
and *The Canterbury Tales*

and then we used to say
his first words would be
"Whanne that Aprill with its shoures soote
the droughte of March hath perced to the roote...."
We told him stories about his grandfather
and how he almost went down
on the last sub sunk in the last war.
And all about his big brother,
who painted a big red flower
and stuck it to the hospital wall
for good luck.
We even told him about his own heroic journey,
and who knows?
Maybe all the stories we hear in our lives
take root somehow,
because when he was seven years old,
before going to school
he'd lie on the couch
waving a massive toy sword in the air
and tell himself stories
about a superhero named
Starchild.

At first we were the only parents
singing and talking on the ward,
but after a while the idea caught on,
and soon the other mothers and fathers
began to talk and sing to their babies,
and the whole place filled up

with lullabies and nursery rhymes,
a river of once-upon-a-times ....

But he wasn't getting better, and he wasn't getting worse,
as if he was hovering between Heaven and Earth,
unsure if he was ready
to be all the way born.
One summer afternoon
I was sitting by the crib as usual,
and as I listened to the incessant beeps
and saw him there so fragile in his sleep
on that particular summer day,
all my fatherly courage went away,
my tongue froze,
I lost all of my stories,
I even forgot how to cry
even though I had tears in my eyes.
I felt so helpless that
I turned to ice.
I sat for a long time
then got up,
left the ward,
left the hospital,
and began to walk
through the crowded streets,
and *Starchild ho,*
Starchild hi,
nothing could touch me
as I walked by.

Walking north up University Avenue
kilometre after kilometre,
west on Davenport,
north again up the ravine
along the dry creekbed,
then I must have turned west on St. Clair
because I found myself
in our own backyard,
and I sat down
in a chair
under the wild plum tree.
And I couldn't move,
couldn't even pick up the phone
or lift the beer
someone put in my hand,
just sat there.
And when the shadows of the tree reached across the
yard
our neighbour walked across the street and said:
"When I was born I almost died.
In fact, I still carry my own death certificate."
And this is the story she told:
When she was born she weighed one pound.
The doctors told her parents she was going to die that
night –
there was no NICU in those days.
Her parents said they wanted to take her home to die.
It was a busy night in a little country hospital some-
where in France –

there were several emergencies going on that night,
so the doctors asked if they could write the death certificate
and come out to the farm the next morning to verify
the death.
Her parents agreed and brought her home.
And her father heated eight big bricks,
wrapped them in blankets,
put them in a circle,
and laid her in the middle
just like a farmer does
with a sick lamb
in the winter.
Her parents waited there all night,
and in the morning
she gave her first cry,
and that's when they knew
she might not die.
And she said:
"I still carry my death certificate to remember how I
came into the world –
Go back and tell your son the neighbours
will give a hell of a party when he comes home."
It was dark when she finished her story.
I got out of my chair,
hugged her,
took the subway back downtown,
and sat by his crib all night long telling jokes,
and the midnight nurses wondered about the strange guy
who was laughing and crying at the very same time.

A few days later he made *his* first cry —
a tremulous squeak,
a tiny squawk,
not much of a cry.
But you should have seen
the mothers and fathers and nurses and doctors
jump for joy —
Starchild has a voice!
Starchild made a noise!
And there was a mighty jubilation on the ward.

That night I told him a new story:
"Starchild, you're not the first one to come into the
world with a cry ...."

Listen ....
They say that at the beginning of the world,
Worldmaker called Sun, Moon, Darkness, and Rain
and said, "I've called you here, my children,
to find out what you will do when I have gone.
The time is coming for me to leave the world I've created.
I will send Heart in my place.
But before I go, tell me your plans."
And the bright, hot Sun replied,
"Worldmaker, I will burn and burn and burn with all
my strength!"
"No," said Worldmaker, "for then you'd destroy the
world I've made.

You'll have to take turns with Rain, and after you've warmed the earth,
Rain will come and refresh it – Rain, what about you?"
"Oh, Worldmaker, I will pour and pour and pour with all my strength!"
"No, Rain – I don't want to drown the earth and all of its creatures.
You must take turns with Sun.
What are your plans, Darkness?"
"Worldmaker, I will rule forever!"
"Ah, no, my child, for if you do, my creatures will never behold the beauty of the world
I have made for them.
Only when Moon is in its last quarter will it be your time to rule.
And, Moon, my strange, sweet child,
I will tell you your fate.
You will circle the world, sometimes round, sometimes thin as a knife blade
flying through the midnight sky,
cutting loose dreams.
And now the time has come for me to leave.
I will send Heart in my place."
And so saying Worldmaker disappeared.

Now, day by day,
there were small signs of improvement.
One day the nasogastric tube came out.
One day the monitors were disconnected,

One day the bruises faded, and he opened his eyes.
The doctors were surprised,
but one of them was particularly wise, and he said,
"Even in the NICU there are many mysteries,
and sometimes the things we don't understand
clear up by themselves,"
and
we
finally
began
to
dare
to
hope.

That afternoon we went to pick up his older brother
from the hospital play lounge.
We stood at the door and watched as he strung beads
on a wire toy—
blue white yellow red
blue white yellow red—
always the same pattern, making his own small order in
the middle of the storm.
He ran over for hugs when he saw us
and showed us a picture he'd made.
"I drew another red flower
for when he comes home."

And now it is the night before

we bring him home.
I sit beside his crib
amid the infants sleeping,
the monitors beeping—
only Starchild is awake,
his eyes opening
at the sound of a familiar voice:
How many miles to Babylon?
Three score miles and ten.
Can I get there by candle-light?
Yes, and back again.
If your heels be nimble and light,
you can get there by candlelight.
Starchild,
we've been here a long time,
and I've told you lots of stories,
but you haven't heard how any of them end.
I wanted you to stick around and listen –
I never even told you what happened to the Johnnycake.

Listen....
The Johnnycake couldn't stay out among the stars forever.
He was coming back towards earth when he rolled by
the river
that stretches between here and there,
way out there at the edge of the world,
and on the riverbank
he met a little red fox.
"Where are you going, Johnnycake?"

"I outran an old man, an old woman,
a cow, a horse, a goat,
the medical personnel of the Hospital for Sick Children,
and I can outrun you, too!"
"Excuse me," said the little red fox,
"I couldn't hear you –
please come a little closer and tell me again."
So the Johnnycake rolled a little closer
and said, "I outran—"
But that's as far as he got.
The little red fox opened up its mouth
and gobbled up that Johnnycake,
and that was the end of the Johnnycake.
But the little red fox still lives happily ever after
on the riverbank
by the edge of the world,
and I guess that we'll all meet *him* one day.

And as for Heart, the story says that
when Worldmaker disappeared Heart came into the world.
Heart was small and red, about the size of your daddy's
closed hand.
And just like you the other day, Heart was crying.
Heart came to Sun, Moon, Darkness, and Rain and said,
"I am weeping because I cannot find the one who made me,
the one who made the world."
And they replied, "We do not know where Worldmaker
has gone."
Heart said, "If you cannot tell me where to find the

One who made the world,
I will enter into Man and Woman, and through them
I will continue my search."
And so Heart jumped into Man and Woman,
and ever since then
every child born of Man and Woman
is born with a longing to meet
the One Who Made the World,
the host of the land where souls come from before
we're born
and return to when we die,
the Mystery of Mysteries.
And we call that longing "Heart."

Starchild,
you're coming home tomorrow.
The house is ready for you.
Your brother made another red flower and taped it over
your crib.
You'll meet three of your grandparents and hear lots of
stories about the fourth one.
The whole neighbourhood is waiting to welcome you
home.
The doctors tell us
they're amazed you made it this far.
They say we'll have to wait for the milestones
to see what kind of human being you'll be.
I guess that just adds to the suspense.
Whatever happens next

I hope you never lose your song
and you always hold on to your stories.
May your heels be nimble and light
so you *can* get there by candlelight.
I hope you keep searching for the One Who Made the
World,
and mind those foxes.

LOCAL 1001

If we modern-day yarnspinners carried cards I'd be a card-carrying member of Local 1001, the International Union of Stormfools. This is the worldwide tribe of artists and tradition-keepers who work as travelling storytellers. We are what my Métis friend Ron Evans calls "stormfools" – storytellers who are willing to travel to any listener in need of a good story. My cousins in Detroit still can't believe this is what my job has been for all these years. "From this you make a living?" they ask. Well, I reply, I live on what I make, which is a bit different than what most people would call a living. It seems amazing to me, too, even after almost forty years of trying. This is a good, even an exhilarating, union to belong to, though we have a long way to go before we ensure a place for storytelling in today's society, let alone a living wage for tellers. We are all, as the proverb says, "making the path by walking it." The pieces in this section chronicle the vicissitudes of working as a professional storyteller. The tall tale at the end–"Stormfool's Cool Gig"–came out of a time when I was waiting to hear about a grant.

It made me wonder how we value stories in the early twenty-first century.

RAISED BY LIBRARIANS

I was raised by librarians. It's like being raised by wolves but wilder. When Toronto's librarians went on strike in 2012, I went down to the picket line by City Hall and told them fairy tales through a megaphone. It was a small way of thanking them for running the greatest municipal library system in the world and, more personally, for turning me into a storyteller.

My love affair with the Toronto Public Library began when I wandered into Boys and Girls House Library in 1972. I had moved to Toronto from California and got a summer job at Bolton Camp. I went to the library to find folk tales to read aloud to my semi-feral campers.

Although I had never worked with kids before, I had spent time in a California jail after protesting the Vietnam war, been bonked on the head by a French cop in Paris after the Russian invasion of Czechoslovakia, hitchhiked the West Coast many times, and studied Homer and Chaucer in university. None of these varied political and scholarly experiences had prepared me for my miniature lords of misrule. Luckily, I discovered, they loved to listen to fairy tales – the longer the better.

One night, as we sat around the campfire, I had a revelation. The counsellor was spinning a yarn about Old Man Bolton. He was our local axe-murdering ghost who, after chopping everybody up, had escaped into the forest surrounding the camp. There, the counsellor quietly told us, Old Man Bolton was still limping around culling stray campers.

I was amazed to see that my boys had been transformed into the world's greatest listeners. A window of time opened, and I understood that my lads hearing summer camp ghost stories were no different than the audience of Greek royalty who heard Homer chant the mighty epics. Even in 1973, the story fire was still burning; the art of storytelling was still alive, and humans – especially my grubby, ardent, hero-hungry boys – had not lost our passion for word of mouth stories.

I was hooked. The problem was, although I wanted to learn the storyteller's mysterious art and even had my own captive audience, I was painfully shy, extremely forgetful, and didn't know any stories.

So I did what people have always done in case of emergency: I went to the library. On my days off, I would drive down to Boys and Girls House and come back to camp with a stack of stories, which I would read aloud at night.

One day that summer, the moment of truth arrived. I'd learned a folk tale in my head and tried telling it to my boys without the book. It began well enough. "Once upon a time there was a king and a queen, and the king went blind. He called his three sons and said, 'Go find a cure for my blindness.'" The first two princes sallied forth, but the third, a lazy, good-for-nothing lad, went out into the garden to nap under his favourite apple tree.

I was just about to tell my boys how this third prince has a hero's dream, when Frankie, my chief trouble-maker, decided it was a good moment to let loose a great and cabin-shaking fart. Pandemonium ensued.

I was so mad that, breaking every rule of camp coun-selling and child-tending, I threw him out of the cabin. Then I continued the story as Frankie banged on the door and yelled that Old Man Bolton was going to chop him up. Despite the commotion, the remaining boys heard how the third prince listened to his dream, rode forth on the quest road, conquered evil, got help from his horse of power, married the fairy firebird, and cured his father's blindness. It's a hell of a story, and my boys – except Frankie – spent the next day retelling it to each other and trying to spot stray firebirds in the woods.

After that summer I became a librarian groupie. My fierce, passionate, story-loving librarians taught me that when a story is told it's more important for the listeners to see the story than the teller. I learned that, in a world where people think memory can be bought on a chip, the word of mouth and the word of heart still matter. You can't double-click on wisdom. Most of all, they taught me that the listener is the hero of the story. My bad boy, Frankie, was the third prince of my story. All the daydreamers, the kids who get sent to the office each day, the unregarded kids from the poorest parts of town – and, yes, even that brat who makes rude noises instead of listening politely – all may have the qualities of a hero, if only we can see it in them. Librarians would never have kicked Frankie out of the story circle. If he doesn't hear the stories, how will he learn that he, too, may one day seek and find his own firebird?

After that summer, Toronto's public libraries became my second home, and the city's librarians my teachers, mentors, and friends. Bolton Camp has since closed down, and Boys and Girls House moved around the corner. Our librarians, in their quiet and courageous way, have made the Toronto Public Library the best in the world. With their encouragement, I filled my head with folk tales and set out on my own storyteller's quest. As for Frankie, I look for him in every audience. I still owe him a fairy tale.

STORING STORIES

Michael Ondaatje is lying on the floor in a box. Next to him – or rather a pile of his most recent book – I see a stack of lobster cookbooks, some gardening manuals, a small case of poetry, and a half-empty box of *Ghostwise: A Book of Midnight Stories*, edited by me. Yes, there on the pallet by the loading dock, its cover a little patch of dark blue in this hangar-huge warehouse, is my book, a collection of stories told in Canada. I am startled to find it here. The wee load of paperbacks looks so exposed and unattended, so frail on the floor, I have a rush of parental feeling. I want to close the flaps of the cardboard box to keep the dust out, to keep away the evil eye. Mind you, I'm also tickled that these dozen or so weren't sitting with a few crates of their mates on a back shelf somewhere down aisle twelve (which reminds me I never found out how many my publisher printed, and what royalties I might expect). It's like seeing your kid somewhere downtown when you're not expecting to – you're proud of his independence, but you want to run up and ask if he has subway fare.

I shouldn't have been so surprised. I had driven up to General Distributing on Steeles Avenue at the northern edge of Toronto to pick up a small order of this very book. I was going to the Yukon the next day; I needed some gift copies, and as usual I'd left things a bit late. Also, I wasn't keen on spending the $10 for a courier's delivery. It's not that I'm cheap, but like most storytellers, I'm not averse to saving a bit of cash. So I drove up to the edge of the outer suburbs, right to Toronto's treeline (past here the subdivisions look awfully bare) to get the books myself.

Do other tellers/writers ever shlep their own books from the warehouse? I highly doubt it. There's no glamour in shouldering a case of literature, even – or perhaps especially – if you're the author or editor. This is nothing like finding your books in a bookstore. That too-rare experience is always gratifying; you know that at least the store owner had the excellent taste to give it shelf space, and you can let yourself dream that maybe some smart, discerning story lover may actually shell out some money for the thing. But a warehouse is quite different.

As I dodge the dollies, I realize I enjoy seeing literature treated like produce at the Ontario Food Terminal. I like this place. People bustling around, trucks and forklifts scooting back and forth, truckdrivers having a smoke on the dock, clerks shuffling invoices, phones ringing, printers clicking, packing tape ripping off spools with that rude noise it makes, a faint smell of burning plastic, the darkhaired woman with the tattoo just leaving on her coffee break. And in the middle of it all: a few copies of my book waiting to be launched into the world.

But it isn't "my" book, of course. It belongs to my late grandfather, who used to tell me the ghost story I put in the introduction. It belongs to the storytellers who wrote their stories down, and beyond them, to the assorted elders who knew them first. Closer to home, my partner thought of the title, my father did some inputting, my mother translated a story from Quebec, my kids listened as I field-tested the stories on them, my friends heard me complain about it for years, my editor and I fought and jubilated over the manuscript. Walter Benjamin once wrote that "the traces of the storyteller cling to the story the way the hand-prints of the potter cling to the clay vessel." When I see the book in its box by the warehouse door, I think of all the handprints and voice-prints it bears, and realize the word of mouth can only be temporarily frozen on a page, caught between the covers of a book.

And that's the pleasure of the warehouse, at least for me. Oral stories are meant to be handled, made use of, passed from tongue to ear, trucked through everyday life to their home made of voice and memory. "Hey, Winston, get me two cases of Grisham and a box of Yashinskys!" "I'm on it, Vijay!" What could be more fun than to see my – our – book hauled off the shelf, plunked on a pallet, and carried to the edge of the loading dock? These stories want out!

WHY STORYTELLERS TALK TO THEMSELVES

Don't be alarmed. In the months leading up to the annual Toronto Storytelling Festival, you may see more than the usual number of your fellow citizens walking around Toronto talking to themselves. This isn't a sign of the spread of handless phone technology, or a phenomenon with public health implications. More likely, these are storytellers rehearsing for an upcoming session. This tendency to talk to ourselves is one of the job hazards of storytelling. I do it all the time, sometimes on long walks through my neighbourhood ravines, sometimes riding my bike to work, and sometimes – although I always feel I should be especially discreet in public places – on the busiest sidewalks. A high collar on my parka helps, or a scarf I can mutter into without attracting attention. I also rehearse in my car, and have often seen alarmed drivers give me a particularly wide berth as they pass me on the 401 (or, if I'm working on an exciting passage, as I pass them).

It can get embarrassing. I was once trying to learn

"The Princess and the Pea." It's short, but the devil to memorize. As I was walking by the Brunswick Tavern in a heavy fog one night, I yelled out, "But she must be a *real* princess!" A surprised woman walked by, shaking her head at my outburst and wondering what kind of princess-loving idiot had just gotten stewed at the Brunnie.

I also get in trouble when I'm going over my lines for "The Miller's Tale," from Chaucer's *Canterbury Tales*. Many years ago, in a burst of literary enthusiasm (and inspired by the greatest Chaucer teacher in the world) I memorized the whole thing, all six hundred lines of rhyming Middle English couplets. I've recited it many times since, usually to an audience of one: myself. My ride to work usually covers about a hundred lines—say, from when Absolon kisses Alisoun's behind ("Abak he sterte, and thoughte it was amyss, for wel he wiste a womman hath no berd; he felt a thyng al rough, and longe yherd ...") to the part when Nicholas, her lover, sticks his tush out the window in the dead of night and blows one directly into the hapless Absolon's face. It's fun for me but strange for the bystanders who hear a guy on a bike chanting Middle English lyrics such as: "This Nicholas let flee a fart as grete as it had been a thonderdent, that with the strook he (i.e., Absolon, the fartee) was almost yblent (blinded)."

Students don't seem to learn poetry by heart any more, let alone folk tales and fairy tales. I think that's a shame, not because I think they should be forced to declaim verse in public, but because it's an eminently useful thing to know poetry and stories in your head. For one thing, you always have a quote ready for any occasion. My friend, Belfast-raised Canadian storyteller Alice Kane, knew thousands of poems, hymns, plays, and stories. Whenever she saw me, she chanted a verse from a Presbyterian hymn: "Dare to be a Daniel, Dare to stand alone, Dare to have a purpose firm, and Dare to make it known!" And whenever I, more than forty years younger, kvetched about my life, she'd always come out with her favourite Irish saying: *'Tis a poor heart that never rejoices.*

A community needs word keepers, people who can keep stories and poems from being forgotten. We've been called many things over the centuries: bards, troubadours, Irish *shanachies*, African griots, tradition-bearers, First Nations elders, yarnspinners, myth tellers, purveyors of bull manure, or just plain storytellers. Our purpose has always been to keep alive the words, ephemeral and powerful at the same time, that can be so easily lost in the rush and distraction of everyday life. Especially *our* everyday lives, here in the early years of the twenty-first century, when we can hoard massive quantities of data but forget our ancestral tales, and when we're only now discovering that we can't double-click on wisdom. So if you see someone walk by muttering and gesticulating, they just might be rehearsing a story, or, if it's me, revelling in Chaucer's magnificent, medieval, irresistible words.

CHAUCER BY HEART

Professor Marvin Mudrick is the reason why I have a particular affection for women's haunche-bones. This little-used term for a woman's thighs comes from a scene in Chaucer's "Miller's Tale," and Professor Mudrick used to recite the passage with great relish and, we all assumed, expert knowledge:

> That on a day this hende Nicholas
> Fil with this yonge wyf to rage and pleye,
> Whil that hir housbonde was at Oseneye,
> As clerkes ben ful subtile and ful queynte,
> And prively he caughte hire by the queynte,
> And seyde, "Ywis, but if ich have my wille,
> For deerne love of thee, lemman, I spille."
> And heeld her harde by the haunche-bones....

I can't vouch for the authenticity of his Middle English accent (I always thought it had a Philadelphia edge to it), but he certainly communicated Chaucer's supremely generous understanding of sex, desire, and good, good lovin'.

I ended up memorizing "The Miller's Tale," all six hundred lines of it, inspired by my friend Ellen Yeomans, another one of Mudrick's students in the late sixties. We were at the College of Creative Studies, at the University of California at Santa Barbara. One hot summer afternoon, a few of us had climbed up Mission Canyon and were skinny-dipping in one of the rock pools by Seven Falls. As we and the salamanders stretched out naked on the smooth stone, Ellen recited the entire hour-long story. When I got back to Toronto, I spent a whole summer jamming every couplet into my faulty memory.

Learning "The Miller's Tale" by heart is one of the most useful things I've ever done. Mudrick had a way of teaching literature that made it feel practical, important, as if novels, poems, and plays carried real weight in the world. As if it mattered that those pilgrims made their way to Canterbury, yarnspinning on the King's Highway; or that Boswell caught and commemorated Dr. Johnson's conversation; or that we ourselves, scratching away at fiction in Mudrick's creative writing classes, were doing something of value, and sometimes something noble.

How is it useful knowing all that Middle English in my head? For one thing, I can recite Chaucer as I swim laps. If I swim a mile, I'm usually climbing out of the pool about the time Alisoun, the carpenter's wife, and Nicholas, the horny student who rents a room in their house, are finally hopping into bed: "and ther was the revel and the melodye." The best use to which I put the poem was when our second son was in the neonatal intensive care unit at Toronto's Hospital for Sick Children. Sitting by his crib telling stories – including bawdy ones – I tried to convince him the world was too beautiful for a short visit. Our son lived, thanks to the doctors and nurses and his own fierce courage, and we've wondered ever since if hearing a non-stop stream of words and stories – especially about love and desire, likerous young women and guys who know they'll spill if they don't get their fill – may have provided the beacon his soul needed to find its way in. Some Buddhists chant Sutras to the dying. Perhaps we need to sing lullabies and tell fairy tales to the fragile babies in the NICU.

Another useful thing about knowing poems in your head is that you've got a stock of quotes that tend to pop up at life's odder moments. Sometimes when I'm not sure where someone is, I remember what the monk told Absolon, Alisoun's unlucky admirer, when he asked where John the carpenter was: "Wher that he be, I kan nat soothly seyn." When I hear a friend has broken up with a lover, I remember what happened when Absolon falls quickly out of love with Alisoun after kissing her, not on her mouth, but in an unexpectedly rough and long yherd place, considerably south of her beautiful face: "His hoote love was coold, and al yqueynt."

Speaking of *queynts*, there are things you learn about a poem or story when you memorize it and say it out loud. As a storyteller, you catch the rhymes and echoes on your tongue, and that opens a new sense of the poem. For example, "The Miller's Tale" may be the only example in world literature of a quadruple entendre. The first entendre of one of Chaucer's favourite words is in the passage I quoted above, when we find out that Nicholas, the horny astrologer-clerk, has figured out his landlord is out of town and that, voila, his gorgeous young wife has just come into his room: "As clerkes ben ful subtile and ful queynte," that is, "cunning," he has planned his assault on her virtue well. In the very next line, just before Nicholas confesses his desire to Alisoun while holding her hard by her haunche-bones, he starts his courtship with a part of her anatomy just above them: "And prively he caughte hire by the queynte." She wasn't too impressed, at least not until he "gan mercy for to crye, and spak so faire, and profred him so faste." We may well imagine just what he was proferring to convince her to become his lover. So the second queynte is what the Wife of Bath sweetly calls her "belle chose." The third entendre shows up when the carpenter, convinced by Nicholas that the flood is coming, runs to tell his beloved Alisoun the bad news. She's in on the plot, of course: "And she was war, and knew it bet than he, what al this queynte cast was for to seye." In this context, it again means something like "ingenious" or "clever." But what a splendid pun—for the trick they're playing on the stupid, jealous husband is indeed all about her queynte. The fourth change Chaucer rings on it comes in the line I quoted above, the one I remember when my friends' hearts are broken, as Absolon's hot love became instantly cold and, graphically, "yqueynt." The same word rhymes with *cleverness*, *cunt*, *ingenious*, and *quenched* and echoes the progress—or lack of it—of the protagonists seeking access to Alisoun's *belle chose*.

When you read it aloud, or tell it from memory, you quickly discover that Chaucer wrote for the ear. Apparently he would read his pieces aloud to the lords and ladies at court. Besides hearing the astonishing music in the language, it seems to me the stories unroll in a cinematic way when you say them out loud. Sometimes you realize that Chaucer has pointed his camera at angles and scenes the words only hint at. For example, after the carpenter has entered Nicholas's room, after breaking down the door with his knave, "who was a strong carl for the nones," he finds Nicholas sitting immobile, just as the knave described (he'd come up earlier and peeked in through a hole at the bottom of the door). After the carpenter exhorts him to wake up and think on God "as we doon, men that swynke"—that is, work—Nicholas says that he'll reveal the terrible secret of the impending aquatic destruction of the world, but only and privately to John. He says, "Fecche me drynke, and after wol I speke in pryvetee of certeyn thyng that toucheth me and thee." As a teller of this story, I know exactly where he's looking as he says this line. Chaucer doesn't spell it out, but if you let your mind's eye dwell on the scene, you'll catch a glimpse of the knave standing over by the now-doorless doorway. How could he tear himself away from the strange mise en scène? He's lurking there, hoping to find out why Nicholas was staring up into the air for two days straight, and especially hoping to hear the revelation that Nicholas has just promised to tell his boss, the good, dumb, hard-swynking carpenter. As he tells the carpenter to bring the beer that his apocalyptic secret requires, he glances over at the hovering, eavesdropping knave. "I wol telle it noon oother man, certeyn," he whispers to John, glaring at the strong carl, who is by now scurrying away, daunted by Nicholas's baleful gaze.

It doesn't matter if this is in the text. Beyond Chaucer's words is the story, the world, if you will, where the various shenanigans of "The Miller's Tale" take place. In Tanzania, the traditional storytellers begin: "I have been and I have seen." Their audience calls back: "See so that we may see." Chaucer doesn't need to tell us where Nicholas is looking because he trusts that we, hearing the tale, are seeing it as fully and richly as our imaginations allow.

Another example of how telling the story releases new meaning comes early on, when we first meet Nicholas. He's a typical student, from the thirteenth or twenty-first century. He likes to jam on a stringed instrument, drink way too much beer, chase girls, dabble in things spiritual, and mooch off his friends. Describing his musical talents, Chaucer tells us:

And al above ther lay a gay sautrie,
On which he made a-nyghtes melodie

So swetely that al the chambre rong;

And Angelus ad virgenem he song;

And after that he song the kynges noote.

Ful often blessed was his myrie throte.

Generations of scholars, apparently, have struggled to figure out just what song "the kynges noote" may be. In the text Mudrick used, *Chaucer's Major Poetry*, edited by Albert C. Baugh, we learn in a footnote that "All attempts to identify this song or tune are unconvincing." However, if you've ever been a student, and sat around drinking beer and playing guitars or sautries, thinking of all the girls in town who might be angels or virgins or likerous eighteen-year-olds, but are, most of them, just plain unavailable, you'll know that this isn't a song at all. It's very likely that Nicholas—after singing his holy, seduction-worthy ballads—let go with a good lonely-guy-in-his-bedroom burp. "The kynges noote" is medieval slang for the slightly subversive rude noise that somehow needs to be expressed just after hymns, ballads, or reverences to distant authorities. Or it could be a fart. But I vote for a traditional undergraduate burp—and when better than after singing, lustily and longingly, Angelus ad virginem. Can I prove my theory? Of course not. But it seems to me true to the scene, to the character, to the story, and to my own memory of student life. So when I recite "The Miller's Tale," I imagine Nicholas's hearty burp. You'll see and hear your own mind-movie, of course.

Professor Mudrick used to teach us that Chaucer was the greatest poet in the history of literature, not only because he dwelled at the very wellsprings of the English language (all of its linguistic streams had come together recently, and are still audible in Middle English), not only because, Mozart-like, he was able to write with humour about terribly serious things; he was the greatest poet because he measured and expressed human life with the greatest and most compassionate moral compass. There was room for everyone on the pilgrimage. One little phrase gives a clue to this moral vision. Nicholas and Alisoun are in the midst of planning the ruse that will buy them a night of amorous bliss. It involves, you'll recall, convincing the carpenter that a flood of Noah-like magnitude is coming, and that he must hang three tubs in the rafters so they can all escape the water. In plotting their trick, while the carpenter was again out of town,

> Hende Nicholas and Alisoun
> Acorded been to this conclusioun,
> That Nicholas shal shapen hym a wyle
> This sely jalous housbonde to bigyle;
> And if so be the game wente aright,
> She sholde slepen in his arm al nyght,
> For this was his desir and hire also.

The scene ends on a purely Chaucerian note. We're reminded that, yes, it was the impetuous Nicholas who initiated this affair, but it is, in fact, a mutual choice of intimacy. Without her sovereign decision to take him as her lover (and we know from the Wife of Bath that "sovereynetee" is the thing that all women most desire), love would not be possible. The last three words—and hire also—come almost as an afterthought, a throwaway line to cap the scene; but in Chaucer's moral universe they become a delicate reminder of the nature of true desire even in the middle of his bawdy yarn.

I was a student at the College of Creative Studies from its first year until 1972. Once I stopped being scared of him, I spent as much time as possible in   Mudrick's classes and office. Chaucer led me to Homer, then on to Icelandic sagas, then into the world of storytelling. That journey has taken me to festivals and gatherings all around the world. I often think that Mudrick, who died in 1986, was like Harry Bailly for his Californian literature students. Harry was the Keeper of the Tabard Inn on the high road to Canterbury, and it is his passion for stories that launches the *Tales*. Seeing this likely group of travellers show up at his inn, he insists that each of them tell their own story—"tales of best sentence and moost solaas"—along the way: "For trewely, confort ne myrthe is noon, to ride by the weye doumb as a stoon." Mudrick believed that a life lived without literature and music and art is indeed to live stoon-doumb.

3RD STORY
STORMFOOL'S COOL GIG

This story came out of a time in my life when I was waiting to hear news about a grant I'd applied for. I kept thinking about how we value stories in our society, and remembering what Angela Sidney used to say: "I have no money to leave my grandchildren. My stories are my wealth." This story is dedicated to all the freelance artists in the world.

I knew it was an unusual gig when I had to wear a silk blindfold in the back of the limo. I figured the chauffeur drove me about an hour out of town. There were lots of turns and twists, and he asked if I preferred air conditioning or an open window. Open window, I said. It smelled good out there, so far from the city. I guess we were on the 401 for about forty-five minutes, then turned off and drove another fifteen or so. He pulled up and used something electronic, a gate opened, and we drove for a few kilometres down a long gravel driveway and finally stopped. I could smell hay and horses. The chauffeur opened my door and said, "You can take off your blindfold, sir."

The farm…or ranch…or estate…I'm not sure what to call it…was huge. I could see fields and forests and bushland and stables right out to the horizon. We were on a slight hill, and I could see that this was all one piece of land, as big as a township. A small river ran in a valley on the other side of the house. The house itself was a graceful, rambling set of buildings made of stone and cedar—I guessed about a hundred years old, but with some very contemporary parts. In fact, I was sure the main house was a Frank Gehry design. It had a solar roof, I was pleased to observe. The whole place had a nice sense of proportion, nothing overshadowing anything else. Sometimes you see these places in the suburbs, subdivisions with monster homes and names like the Vales of Castlemore, and you wonder about their weird turrets and stone lion gateposts and five-car garages. Lots of money, not much taste. But this place made me happy, just seeing the materials and proportions. I was enjoying the vista so much, I almost forgot that I didn't even know why I had been brought here.

The chauffeur cleared his throat and, with a smile, led me up the wheelchair ramp to the front door. I was happy to see the ramp. I don't need it myself, but I never tell stories in places my friends in wheelchairs can't go. He opened it and nodded me in. I was pleased by his courtesy. I can't say that as a working storyteller I encounter this every day. More typically, I show up at a school and wait in the staff room until I do my show. The good schools, of course, offer staff room coffee.

The bad ones leave you sitting there until showtime. The good schools do introductions like this: "Boys and girls, we're honoured and delighted to welcome Stormfool to our school. You're going to have a wonderful time listening to his stories." The bad schools have someone say: "You'd better behave and not make a sound—or else you'll be sent straight to the office. It was disgraceful how this school acted when the musician came last month. We'll be watching. Billy, that means you. In fact, Billy, come with me. You'll spend the hour in my office." Then the teachers take out their grading. I don't let them, of course; the written word, I tell them in a nice way, is banned during a storytelling performance. Before I leave the school, I always stop in to the office to tell Billy his own story. "Hey, dude," I whisper, "you're the hero of every fairy tale...." That usually makes him smile, even if the v-p is frowning across her desk at us.

We walked down a long hall. We passed a Picasso, two Chagalls, a Giacometti, and—I stopped to look more closely—three Rembrandts. At the end of the hall we came to a bedroom. It was dimly lit, with the shades half-drawn. There was an old man in bed. He was wearing dark glasses. From the way he kept his head poised, as if to pick up all the echoes coming his way, I had a feeling he was blind.

"Stormfool," he said in a quiet, clear voice. "Welcome. I'm honoured that you came to see me." When I heard his voice, I recognized him. We used to hear that distinctive voice—strong but never loud—on television and radio. Now I knew why the blindfold had been required. The man in the bed was probably the richest man in the world, a billionaire many, many times over. He was also the world's most famous recluse. He hadn't been seen in public for many years. He had gone into a self-imposed exile when his only child, a daughter, was killed in a botched kidnapping. Then his wife died of a broken heart. Then he simply disappeared. Mostly the world seemed to respect his choice of absolute privacy. It had all happened a long time ago. A wave of grief came over me, thinking about what he'd been through, and a wave of relief, too, as I thought about my own two boys. I guess that's one benefit of being a freelance storyteller—no one will ever try to kidnap your kids and hold them for ransom.

"Thank you for coming," he said. "I apologize for the blindfold, but we've found that it's simpler that way. Would you like some tea or coffee?"

"Coffee sounds good." He had an old-fashioned sense of hospitality that I immediately warmed to. I still wasn't sure why I was here, but storytellers tend to be good listeners. I was in no rush. You know what they say: Some people have the watches, but the storytellers have the time. And it was certainly the best coffee I'd ever had in my life. I did have to pick up my boys from their mother later that evening, but it was still mid-afternoon.

"As you can see," he began, "I don't get around much any more. I'm blind, I'm old, and I'm dying. I'm not afraid of dying. As you may know, I lost long ago those who were most precious to me. I look forward to joining them soon. As for material possessions, I've made all the money and bought all the things I'll ever need or want. But now that I'm nearing the end of my life, I keep remembering how things were before I became rich. You see, I grew up poor, in a village on an island so remote we didn't have electricity until I was a teenager, when the American army set up a base nearby and brought the benefits of so-called civilization. I had a wonderful childhood. At night, there was a storyteller in the village, and we'd all gather around the fire to listen to him. He knew thousands of stories—creation myths, legends of the island, chronicles of every family. He even saved our lives once with his stories.

One day when I was a boy we saw the sea begin to withdraw. It pulled back to the horizon, and we were all about to rush out and collect shells from the seabed when he called to us and said, 'No. I remember a story from many years ago. The sea ran away from the land, and then a wall of water came back. Run for the high ground.' Such was the honour and respect we had for him that we all listened. When the tsunami hit the island an hour later, nobody died. His story saved us all, even though the last tidal wave had happened more than a hundred and fifty years before. He knew all of his listeners, and would choose his stories to fit the people around the fire. He had nicknames for all of us. He used to call me the Golden Traveller—I guess he knew I'd be leaving the village to find my fortune, and so it turned out. I left, and became the man you've probably read about. And now that my travels are over, I've come to realize that as rich as I am, I felt richer when I sat around that fire listening to the old storyteller.

"Stormfool, I want to hear stories again. Not on a television or computer or radio, but straight from the mouth of a real storyteller. We live in strange times. We have so many ways to communicate today, and so little to say. The television and Internet know so many stories, but the old storyteller in my village knew me. I want to hear stories again, and that's why I asked you to come today. I'd like to offer you a job. I want you to be my storyteller."

"How did you choose me?" I asked.

"We do our research," he said. The chauffeur had brought in some snacks, and laughed gently when he heard that. "Lots of research," he added. "We've been following your career for a long time. We know about how you used to live up north, and travel around telling stories even in the worst weather. We know about that time you left the concert hall in Graz, Austria, and told stories to the Turkish kids in the park nearby. They didn't speak English and you didn't speak German or Turkish, but somehow they understood your stories. We know about the time you left the conference in Regina, Saskatchewan, and dropped in to the hospital for handicapped children. We even know about the frogs on the pond in Santa Barbara, California, and how they gathered on lily pads while you played your ocarina and practiced telling stories to them. We know how you became a 'storm fool.'"

They *had* done their research. I got my name– Storm-fool–when I lived up north and went around to little communities telling stories. Even in bad blizzards, I'd head out to visit people who were storm-stayed on their traplines, and tell them fairy tales, myths, long creation stories–just to give them courage and to let them know they weren't alone. They began to call me their "storm fool" and the name stuck. All my life, I've liked to find listeners in unlikely places, though I never dreamed I'd find a place like this. I do most of my storytelling in the poor parts of town. But I was very intrigued by the whole idea. I felt strangely comfortable with him, even though rich people normally make me nervous. They always seem to be ranking you, calibrating by fine degree your place in the social hierarchy, figuring out if they should look down on you or suck up to you. Maybe it's how I grew up. My parents were socialists in the States in the fifties. I was what's called a "red diaper" baby. While my schoolmates were watching TV wrestling and Batman, I was walking picket lines. Apparently my first full sentence was "Hell no, we won't go!" except it wasn't about the war in Vietnam; it was a protest about my bedtime. "Well, I may be able to do that," I said. "I'm more used to trav-elling around, but I could stay put for a change. What would the job involve?"

"Bring your stories here when I need them."

"When would you need me to start?" I asked. Then I realized it was a silly question. The man was dying. He needed to hear stories now. This was a case of emergency storytelling.

"I'd like you to start as soon as possible. Now I know that someone doing such valuable work can't afford to do it for free. What would you charge me to be my storyteller?"

Then I said something a bit foolish. I've never been good with money. I said, "Look, if I decide to try this out, you don't have to pay me anything. I do lots of freebies. I'd be more than happy to come up sometimes and tell stories. I'd do it in honour of the storyteller you grew up listening to."

He nodded and continued. "Thank you for your kind offer. If you decide to be my storyteller, I will accept the gift of your storytelling. And I would like to offer you a gift in exchange. I would like to give you one million dollars per year, not as a fee but as a gift to you. Would you accept it?"

I'm proud of my reaction at that moment. I didn't faint. I didn't fall on my knees and do multiple obeisances at his feet. I didn't burst into tears—that came later, when I got home. Inside, I was yelling: A million dollars! Dude, for that kind of money I'll be your medieval troubadour, your Scandinavian skald, your African griot, your Irish *shanachie*, your praise-singer, your bard, your wondersmith, your granny and grandpa rolled into one, your Native elder, your 24/7 yarnspinner, your speed-dial

dial-a-story, your personal oral narrative resource centre. I'll learn every folk tale, wondertale, creation myth, legend, fable, and joke ever told. Hell, I'll even do your goddam, dishes! I mean, I'd finally have a dental plan! My kids could get their teeth fixed! I was thinking all of that, but what I said was: "Can I let you know on Monday? I didn't bring my calendar today." To tell you the truth, I was a little ashamed to admit that I hadn't been working much at all. The phone just hadn't been ringing except for Revenue Canada wanting the taxes I owed, and Visa wanting me to settle my horrible bill. After all those years of freelancing, I was even thinking of getting a part-time job. Maybe I wouldn't need to, after all.

"Of course." He looked very tired and wan. I could tell our conversation had exhausted him. I looked over at the chauffeur, who nodded. A signal. "Monday," he murmured. "I do hope you will accept. And please take this small honorarium to thank you for coming so far to see me today." He indicated an envelope on the bed, which I picked up. His hand touched mine for a moment, and he held it lightly and warmly the way blind people sometimes do. When he let go, I left.

The chauffeur drove me home. I put on the blindfold without being reminded. Before I drove over to get the boys, I sat in my kitchen. I opened the envelope. There was five thousand dollars in it—more money than I'd made in the previous three months. And then to think I could soon be making a million a year. That's when I started to cry. I felt like a character in one of my own stories: like Ti-Jean when he finds the red and green and blue piglets in the barn, or Ma'aruf the cobbler when he discovers the treasures under the peasants's field, or Ali Baba when he speaks the magic two words that open the robbers' cave. Open sesame! O, yes-a-me! I felt like Yankele, the poor Jew who gets a wish from an angel. Do you remember that story? He only gets one wish. The problem is, he's broke, he and his wife have no children, and his mother, who lives with them (and that can be a problem in itself), is old and blind. What should he do with only one wish and three big *tsuris*, three big troubles? Then he knows. He tells the angel, "I wish that my mother could see her grandchild rocking in a golden cradle." But even all of my stories hadn't prepared me for this blast of good fortune. It was better than getting a Canada Council senior artist grant, better than a MacArthur Fellowship, better—and I mean way better—than inheriting the estate of someone you love.

It's like this.

You spend your life practicing a difficult, little-known, underpaid art.

You do it because when you were young, your Bubbe used to tell you stories about the war, and how she escaped the Nazis. They got the rest of her family, may they rest in peace, but she escaped, thank God. So you feel that if you lose the story frequency, your family will disappear a second time.

Then, when you're a little older, you begin to read

books of folk tales and fairy tales, you read Greek and Norse mythology, you read *The Iliad* and *The Odyssey*, and all about the days long ago when Homer travelled from court to court telling his great stories and always finding a welcome wherever he went. And this is so romantic, you begin wishing that there were still bards and troubadours nowadays, just like there were in Homer's time.

And that's when you understand that your own Bubbe was just as brave as Odysseus, even though she had no Ithaca to return to. And you understand that your Bubbe was a bard in a babushka, and that the oral tradition never really died.

And then your wish, as wishes do, turns into a belief that someone should make sure storytellers come back, even in our society of instant downloads and a thousand channels. But who will that person be? And how can they do it?

And then, in your mid-twenties, you walk into a bank and wait in line and get up to the counter, and you see a sign that changes your life. The teller has just closed, and she puts a sign up that says: NEXT TELLER. And you're hit by the irresistible, undeniable truth that that sign is for you. It's like the old saying: What's for you won't go by you. *You* will have to be the next teller. You are the "one," just like in that movie *The Matrix*: "You are the One!" You'll have to become a storyteller, despite your shyness, your shitty memory, the fact you don't know any stories and aren't sure anybody'd want to listen to you even if you did. And just before you freak out with this almost-unbearable—but still exhilarating—truth, you remember what your Romanian Bubbe used to say when people asked her for the recipe for her famous cake. "It starts like this," she'd say. "Steal two eggs." In other words, improvise. Make it up as you go along. Make the path by walking it. As the Gaelic proverb says: Every force evolves a form. Well, the force of storytelling is certainly with you—now it's a question of finding the forms.

So you begin experimenting, you try and try and try, and fail and fail and fail, trying to figure out how to be a storyteller in the twenty-first century. And slowly, slowly the egg grows legs and learns to walk, as the Chinese say. Slowly, slowly you become a storyteller. And that's when you start to hear rumours about other people around the world doing the same thing, storytellers in Sweden and Singapore and Sao Paulo, in Wales and Whitehorse, in Tel Aviv and Ramallah and Toronto and Tennessee, in Montreal and Chartres and Vancouver—all of them trying to figure out this ancient, avant-garde art, all of them trying to invent a future folklore. And now you know you're not alone, because you're part of an international renaissance, part of the noble company of yarnspinners and wondersmiths. And you're jubilant! Scheherazade lives! We're not an endangered species! The storytellers are back! Homer is in the house! And you're so proud to be part of this tribe of crazy artists, even though you're still making less than the guy who shovels polar bear shit at the zoo.

And all this time, while I was busy learning folk tales and becoming a stormfool, my friends were becoming doctors, lawyers, engineers, computer scientists, professors. They drove new cars, and I drove a twenty-year-old Ford. Oh yes, I did become a very rich man, if you consider stories a form of wealth. But by every other measure of social success, I have always been a stone-broke loser. You know the old proverb: Poverty is no disgrace, but it sure is inconvenient when you need to buy something. Whenever I'd meet my American cousins at bar mitzvahs or weddings, they'd ask the inevitable question: "So from this storytelling you can make a living?" Over the years, I'd perfected my answer: "No—but I live on what I make."

Do you know what kept running through my mind as I sat in the kitchen? I wouldn't have to withdraw sixty or eighty dollars at a time from the friggin' bank machine! I could finally withdraw the princely sum of two hundred dollars and not be scared there wouldn't be enough for food or school supplies the next day. And I also thought: I can finally pay my library fines! I had so many books of folk tales and fairy tales overdue that I used to go to different branches all over the city because I was too embarrassed to run into the librarians where I owed so much in fines. There are almost a hundred library branches in my city, and, in my shame, I visited all of them.

Finally I staggered to my feet, wiped my eyes, and drove over to my ex-wife's place. As I drove, I thought: A new car! I could finally get a decent car! The boys gave me their usual happy hugs, and she gave me her usual wary hug. We had stayed friendly, and we were still attracted to each other. Attracted? Hell, I was still in love with her, and I suspected she might have felt the same way about me, despite all of her dating. It's a funny thing. I couldn't tell her my huge news that night, not on the doorstep. I'm too much of a storyteller to give away such a good punchline without waiting for the proper moment. We storytellers and professional poker players have a saying: Never play an ace when a two will do. Storytelling is the art of peek-a-boo. You have to know when to peek and when to "BOO!" It's like the time I met a bus driver in Pittsburgh, when I was trying to get downtown from the airport. He told me he'd won $50,000 and a trip to Las Vegas by being a contestant on a show called *Wheel of Fortune*. After he won, though, he didn't tell his children, his brothers and sisters, his fellow bus drivers, or even his mom. Only his wife knew what had happened. I asked him why, and he told me that the show was taped, and he wanted them to see him win on television two months later. Imagine holding on to a secret like that! And here I was, not ready to tell my ex-wife about my million dollar salary! Maybe in a day or two, with the kids at a babysitter, a bottle of excellent French wine, a box of Belgian chocolates....

I told the boys about the five thousand dollars, and we had pizza back at my place. Not the usual cheese and tomato version, but the superdeluxe, with everything on it. We thought afterwards that maybe pineapple and anchovies aren't the best combo, but we couldn't resist going wild with my five grand. We went to the mall on Saturday, and they each got new running shoes. Me, too. Then we walked around the rest of the day staring in admiration at our feet.

I paid off my library fines, finally got cable, and put a down payment on a decent—though still used—car. I felt a little drunk with all that cash! And I still had half of my honorarium left!

By Sunday night it dawned on me that I might not be cut out to be a millionaire. I couldn't even blow through five thousand unexpected bonus dollars. But although I wasn't very good at spending money, I certainly didn't mind trying to learn. I reminded myself of the old Romany proverb: A millionaire is someone who has spent a million dollars.

On Monday, after I dropped the boys off at school, there was a knock at the door. I wasn't surprised to see the chauffeur. "I'm in," I said.

We drove north. Those two words, just like Ali Baba's magic, rock-cracking spell, changed my life. I put on the blindfold, and we drove up to the farm.

My listener—that's how I referred to him for the time I worked for him—was truly happy to hear I'd accepted his offer. There was no question of a contract, of course. I knew he was a man of his word. So are storytellers, for that matter. Even though we use fiction, there's always a truth at the heart of every story. It's like the old saying:

The dreamer awakes.
The shadow goes by.
The cock is a myth.
The tale is a lie.
But ponder it well,
Fair maiden, good youth.
The tale is a lie.
The teaching is truth.

I wasn't sure what story to tell. so I sat for a long time in his room, waiting for a story to gather in my mind. The light over the fields was soft and golden— this was early fall. There's an interesting moment just before a storyteller chooses his or her tale. All the old-timers know about this. It's the moment when, of all the stories you know, one comes into your mind as the right story to tell this particular listener at this particular time. I often don't choose stories ahead of time, because, even if it can be a bit nerve-wracking, I enjoy the suspense of this moment. You've probably heard about the rabbi who was renowned for his storytelling ability. He always seemed to have the right story for any moment that arose in life. His student, marvelling at the rabbi's great skill, once asked him what the secret was. How did he know what story to tell, and when, and to whom? How could he learn that technique? The rabbi, not surprisingly, answered: "That reminds me of a story!" And went on to say:

There was once a young man who went off to become a great sharpshooter. He studied for years, mastering every skill of marksmanship. Finally, graduating at the top of his class, he wanted to ride home and show his parents and friends his fantastic ability. As he was riding along, he passed through a little village. On the side of the road was a broken-down barn. On the side of the barn, somebody had painted one hundred targets. And, to the young man's amazement, in the middle of each target, someone had shot a perfect bull's eye. He couldn't believe his eyes. Reining in his horse, he stared and stared at this incredible sight. Then he looked around the poor village. He called out, "Who has done this great feat? Where is the world's greatest sharpshooter?" A little girl walked across the road. "I did it," she said, scuffling her shoes in the sand. "You?" he said. "I can't believe it. I've studied for years, I've learned every skill of sharpshooting, but even I could never do such a thing. What's your secret, little girl?" "Let me explain," she said. "You see, I don't draw the target first. First I shoot, then I draw the target."

The storytelling rabbi explained to his student that it was the same with him. There was no special technique involved. You begin by falling in love with stories. Then you hunt and gather them by reading, by listening, by inventing. You fill your head with stories. Then, as you go through life with a headful of good stories, it's never hard to find a moment to draw the story around.

Suddenly I knew what to tell him. He had lived

through so much danger and sorrow; he had lost so many things dear to him. I remembered a really strange folk tale about that.

Once, long ago, a man left his home and took a long journey. He was gone for many months. On his way back into town, he ran into a neighbour. "How are you doing?" he asked.

"Not too bad. How 'bout you?"

"'Bout the same. I've been away awhile. Any news?"

"Nah, it's been real quiet around here. Not much has happened since you left."

"Are you sure nothing's happened while I've been gone?"

"Well, now that you mention it, your dog died."

"My dog? How did that happen?"

"He got into the barn and ate some burnt horse meat."

"What was burnt horse meat doing in my barn?"

"When your barn burned, all the horses died in the fire."

"You mean to say my barn burned while I was away?"

"Yep. Apparently a spark from the house caught it."

"My house was on fire too?"

"They say it was the candles in the living room burning the curtains."

"But what were candles doing in my living room?"

"They were all around the coffin."

"You mean someone died while I was gone?"

"That would've been your mother-in-law. The shock carried her away."

"What shock was that?"

"Hearin' the news about your wife."

"And what happened to my wife?"

"Oh, I guess she ran away with the gardener."

"My wife ran away, my mother-in-law died, the house burned, the barn burned, the horses died, my dog died—and you told me not much had happened while I was gone!"

Now, you may wonder why I chose to tell that particular story to a man who was dying, and who had suffered as much as my listener. I'm not quite sure, but the strange thing was he laughed and laughed as he listened to this catalogue of disasters. He laughed and kept repeating, "Not much had happened while I was gone...."

He didn't ask for another story that day, and thanked me for coming. I had imagined I'd be there for hours every day, telling long and involved stories to keep him occupied. But the chauffeur gave me a nod, and I said, "Goodbye, my listener."

"Goodbye, my Stormfool. Your story was a good gift."

On the drive back the chauffeur told me my listener hadn't laughed like that for a long time. I was feeling a bit shocked. I'd done some calculating and realized my five-minute story had earned me about four thousand dollars. By the end of the first week of working there, I'd earned twenty thousand. And that was my life for the next weeks and months.

Some days I told short stories, some days I would spin long and elaborate wondertales, stories that took many hours to unfold. I spent October and part of November telling Icelandic sagas. In December he wanted to hear the *Iliad* and the *Odyssey*.

Sing in me, Muse, and through me tell the story
Of that man skilled in all ways of contending,
The wanderer, harried for years on end,
After he plundered the stronghold
On the proud height of Troy.

Then we did short fables, silly stories, and dirty jokes for a few weeks to recover from the epics.

The way he listened, as if the mind-movies he was seeing were real and immediate and breathlessly interesting, reminded me of a boy I once knew, many years ago, a boy who used to listen to his Bubbe telling him about her life as an orphan during the war, and coming to Sweden, and finally settling in Detroit. That little boy was me. I would listen to my grandmother for hours. Most of her stories were true, and the ones that weren't, should have been.

I told my listener about the time my Bubbe was speeding and got pulled over. The young cop said, "Ma'am, you were doing one hundred in a fifty-mile-an-hour zone."

My bubbe said, "I know."

"Where's your driver's licence?"

"I don't have one. I'm legally blind."

"Where are the registration papers for your car."

"I don't have any papers. It's not my car."

"Whose car is it?"

"I don't know," said my Bubbe. "I stole it."

The young cop was amazed. "You stole it? From who?"

"From whom. Do I know? I killed him and stole the car."

"What!"

"Yeah. And I cut up the body and put it in the trunk."

He backed away from my Bubbe and radioed for help. He explained the situation to the senior officer who pulled up. The senior officer went to talk to my Bubbe.

"Open the trunk!"

"Okay." She popped the trunk.

He looked in. Just a spare tire and some old grocery bags.

"Ma'am, is this your car?"

"Of course it is, Officer. Here are the registration papers." She handed them to the police officer. They were all in order.

"Do you have a driver's licence?"

"Why wouldn't I have a driver's licence?" She gave it to him.

"Well, I'm so relieved," he said. "My partner told

me you'd stolen the car, murdered the driver, chopped up his body, and put it in the trunk!"

"Yeah? He probably told you I was speeding, too."

I used to listen to her tell her stories, some tragic, some funny. I guess I knew from a young age that a story doesn't need to have happened to be true. When I asked her about her encounter with the police, she said, "Let's just say that the true part is you should always have a good story to tell, just in case."

It was in early spring that I told my listener a beautiful long wondertale about a young prince who finds a golden feather on the road and picks it up, and it leads him after many adventures to a firebird. He finds love and joy. After a long time, my listener said, "I found my firebird, too." And he told me about his wife and daughter. Not about their deaths, but about their life together. But that was the only time he told me his story.

I spent a year going to the farm, telling my listener stories. But the time came when we both knew he was going to die soon. One afternoon I was telling him stories of Hodja Nasrudin, the wise fool of the Middle East, and I ended with the story about the time Hodja went on a mission of social justice. He told the other villagers that it was unfair that so few people owned so much land and money, while the rest of the world went hungry. He was going on a mission to ensure that all the money in the world was shared equally and justly between the rich and the poor. After a few months people asked him how it was going. "Very well," he said, "I'm ninety-nine per cent done. All of the poor people said yes."

My listener laughed, but then he said, "My Storm-fool, your story is bitter and sweet. I have been much better at making my billions than at sharing them. I have made a decision. I am going to die soon. I will finally be reunited with my firebirds. And when I die, you will inherit all of my fortune. Storytellers know that stories gain value only when you give them away. This philosophy may work for money, too. I only ask that you use my wealth to bring as much happiness to the poor of the world as your stories have brought me. My chauffeur will be well provided for, and all of my employees. But you are the one who will decide what to do with my money."

I was pretty surprised by this turn of events. After a long silence, I said, "Thank you, my listener. I'm honoured by your decision. It reminds me of another story." I didn't know it would be the last story I told him.

There was once a man and a woman who had much land and many cattle, but they had no children. They prayed for a child, and one day an old woman came to their door.

"Bring me millet flour and water," she said. She made a child out of millet paste, and when it dried and hardened she gave it to the man and woman. "Take good care of this doll-child, and let no harm come to it. Teach it your family histories, and give it a secret name. You will have a real child one day."

The woman took good care of the doll-child, but

one day as she was cleaning it, it slipped from her hands and broke in two. "I have broken my child!" she cried. She tried to reconnect the pieces but could not. Nine months later she gave birth, but the parents' joy turned to grief when they saw she had given birth to twins. Back then, in that place, my listener, twins were taboo. Human beings always seem to have something or someone too different to be allowed in. They were considered a fearful curse on the village, and the parents knew that there would be some who would certainly want to kill their children.

They took them deep into the forest and raised them secretly for six years. But things didn't go well in that land, and whenever a cow died or the rains didn't fall, the people whispered about a secret curse. The parents knew their children would soon be discovered and killed. The father went to the forest and led his boy and girl to a waterfall. At the bottom was a great pit. He threw them in and returned to his wife, and both of them wept and wept.

But the boy and girl did not drown. They were swept away by the water to an underground country with a blue sky like ours, and fields and rivers and valleys. It was beautiful, but the people and animals there were all broken in some way. They had broken wings or broken legs or broken hearts. They were blind or deaf or unable to speak.

Yet they were cheerful, and they welcomed the twins.

"Where are we?" they asked.

"This is the country of the broken ones. All of us were thrown away by the world above. Please stay with us. We will take care of you."

And so they stayed, and they were happy there.

One day, when they were playing by a hill, a crack opened in the rock. Their father was weeping on the other side.

"Father, father," they cried. They climbed through the crack and went home with him. Their mother had grown old with grief, but she was happy when she saw her children return. They treated them well, the twins, and never scolded or punished them.

But the children were never happy. "We don't belong in this world anymore," they whispered to each other. They left the house one night holding hands, and they followed the trail that led back to the waterfall.

The twins called out, "Farewell, Mother and Father. We are sorry, but we belong with the creatures who have been broken and thrown away. We are not comfortable in your world anymore. There is not enough room for the broken ones." And they jumped into the pit and were swept away, and their parents never saw them again.

We sat quietly after the story was told. Then I said, "I will try to use your money to make a world where even the broken ones are not thrown away."

My listener nodded and held out his hand. He had tears rolling down his cheeks. "I have enjoyed your stories, my Stormfool," he said.

"And I have enjoyed telling them to you, my listener." I brought his hand to my face so he could touch the tears on my cheeks. When we drove back to the city, I didn't put on my blindfold, and the chauffeur didn't ask me to.

The next morning, the chauffeur drove to my house to tell me my listener had died during the night. He'd been murmuring, "And you told me not much had happened while I was gone," and, "He probably told you I was speeding...." He had died laughing.

My ex-wife and I had been getting along better. She liked the fact that I'd finally gotten a decent job. I might even have proposed getting back together, but I could tell she wasn't quite ready to give up dating. Anyway, that night, I went over to her place with a bottle of excellent wine, and we drank it, and she ate some chocolate, and she led me upstairs. After we had some fun, I told her about my inheritance. Then I gave it all to her. I threw in what was left of my million dollar salary, too. I had hardly spent any of it, except for buying a few cases of single malt and a few boxes of Cuban cigars. And, of course, I got the kids' teeth fixed. We had a lovely evening together – the kids were at a babysitter – but I won't go into the details. See, I figured that my ex-wife would know the best thing to do with the money, and I think you'll agree that she did a good job.

Some of what happened next you know about from the newspapers, or just by looking around. You can thank my ex for things like world peace; clean water; clean air; sustainable agriculture; the return of the North Atlantic cod and the Pacific salmon; the increasing dolphin, bumblebee, and frog populations; and recyclable Palestinian beach balls. Yes, it was her investment that helped them build that recyclable beachball factory in Gaza, and helped transform the whole region into an economic powerhouse. She also used the money to invest in electric cars, and that's why even in Mexico City, Sao Paulo, Nairobi, and Los Angeles you can breathe the air and see the sunset. Exxon wasn't happy about this, of course, but she bought the company and found new jobs for most of the employees, working as unionized tree planters in Canada's national forests.

Here's how she bought world peace. She offered to assume and forgive all the debts of any country that had the same percentage of women in parliament as they had in the population. It was an offer no country could refuse. Now a good deal of the world's parliamentary debates have to do with education, nutrition, and social justice. The shift to women leaders is often cited as the reason that Africa and Central America have become so prosperous. And, of course, that's why governments stopped sending their young men off to slaughter each other in the name of a particular patch of ground, religion, or political system. The big weapons manufacturers weren't happy, of course, but she bought the companies and retrained their employees as early childhood educators. Oh, there are still some companies that make jet fighters, but just for air shows. You have to admit there's something wonderfully thrilling about those jets doing loop-de-loops and hearing the roar of their afterburners kick in on a steep climb. And there are lots of former soldiers leading very competitive capoeira groups. You can watch them practice in your local park.

Since my ex wouldn't go anywhere that wasn't wheelchair accessible, you can imagine how quickly restaurants, schools, libraries, banks, and public transportation all over the world built ramps and elevators. And she founded the Indigenous Languages and Storytelling Project, and now so many of the world's languages are being taught again. Our two sons speak English, French, Hebrew, Arabic, and Ojibway. And, of course, every classroom in the world now has its own handmade, brilliantly coloured talking stick for the storytelling curriculum unit.

I know they say money can't buy love, but in my ex-wife's case she bought clean water, wholesome food, world peace, decent housing for everybody, and restored wetlands, not to mention supporting a feminist revolution. I think she's done well with the money. And, strangely enough, the more she spends, the more she makes. Turns out social justice is good for business. That's why Co-opoly has become the most popular board game in the world.

As for me, what with her busy philanthropy and my storytelling, we don't see each other much these days. I'm back on the road again, but I swing by sometimes to see her and the kids. They're helping her run the foundation. She usually sends me a bit of money now and then, whenever I call to remind her. But my cellphone is pay as you go, and I ran out of minutes a few gigs ago, then I lost my charger. It's all right: I'll be heading home soon enough. Stormfools are like the proverbial bad penny: We always show up. Besides, I'm a very rich storyteller; I just don't have any money.

FUTURE FOLKLORE:
THE STORYTELLER AS CITIZEN

There's a story going around that when Stalin wanted to destabilize the Ukraine, he brought all the region's storytellers together for a feast and then had them killed. He knew that storytellers are often subversive. Folk tales teach us that the bullies of the world must be resisted, even if all you have to fight with are words. The pieces in this section are about times when storytelling intersected with events, people, and places in the wider world. I like to think that, in our own quiet way, the stories we tell make their own subversive and transformative difference in the world we inhabit.

THE TORONTO BOOK OF THE DEAD

I once heard someone ask our beloved Dr. Hugh Morgan Hill how he turned into Brother Blue. Blue answered (and he'll forgive my raggedy memory) something like this: "The reason I put on my bells, butterflies, ribbons, and balloons is that one day I might be walking down the street and there's a man in a house who wants to die. He looks outside and sees a crazy one-man carnival going by, and he says to himself, 'Man, I thought *I* had it bad!' and he decides not to kill himself. I tell stories to keep people from committing suicide."

Thus spake Brother Blue, one of our greatest story-tellers and maybe the world's only bebop praise singer. Sto-rytelling was, for him, an act of service as much as an art.

I remembered Blue's comment about three years ago, when I was trying something I'd never done before. In the middle of a wakeful night, I started to wonder what it would be like to tell a completely fresh, new story, woven from the moment. I had done this with my kids sometimes, spinning a yarn that featured themselves as the heroes, and noticed how much they seemed to enjoy it. But what about doing it with an audience?

I've always loved the camp counsellor in Salinger's story "The Laughing Man." Every afternoon he improvised a story for his boys, all about a great detective known as the Laughing Man. What a great gift – to be able to weave a story on the spot. I admire people in books and in real life who can do this, but I hadn't ever tried it. My discipline, learned from children's librarians like Alice Kane and tradition-loving masters like Joan Bodger, is based on getting a text well and truly learned, and then telling it to others. Sometimes that text is one I've written or adapted, sometimes it is one I've learned from another teller or from a book, but there is always a set of words I have to get right to be able to tell the story. What would it be like making it up on the spot?

And what kind of listener might enjoy such a new, fresh, never-told-before story? At that point Blue's philosophy of storytelling came to mind, and I started to think that a listener in need of a new story would be someone who had stopped hearing his own stories, someone who was no longer wondering what was going to happen next. This person might need a new tale to open their ears, especially if it felt like it was being told just for them.

Many years ago I'd read a terrible news story in *The Globe and Mail*. A young man had jumped in front of a subway train here in Toronto. His father, on his way to the city morgue to identify the body, came to the Rosedale bridge and leapt to *his* death on the tracks below.

This tragic city story had haunted me for years. I decided that my new story would be dedicated to the son and his father. I would try to make up the kind of story that might have kept the young man from killing himself, and might, posthumously, commemorate the father's grief-stricken deed. I called this story "The Toronto Book of the Dead." Because I would be improvising the tale, I called the process *Scheherajazz*. The next day I put up flyers throughout the University district. It read: "I am hunting/gathering a new story. It will be told in memory of a citizen who was too late to save the life of someone he loved."

For seven Tuesday nights, I – with members of the seven different audiences – created a story (which ended up including dozens of stories) in memory of the father and son. It was a kind of citizens' vigil, an observance more than a performance, an honouring of whatever unimaginable pain drove this pair to their respective suicides. On the first night, I said that we were creating a seven-week/seven-chapter "medicine bundle" of stories. The theory is that nobody would kill himself if he were listening to the right story, if he were waiting to hear what happened next. Nobody would choose to leave the room or the world if he were in suspense about the hero's fate, especially if he knew the story was about himself.

"The Toronto Book of the Dead" was spoken and written. After each evening, whoever had made a contribution wrote it down in a folio-sized book. We met in a small back room at the now-gone Café Verité downtown. Somebody should one day write a history of small back rooms in cafés where no one table leg is the same length as any other, and where teenagers come to drink strong black coffee and discuss philosophy. Such places incubate all manner of art, including storytelling. I had a few "props": a golden feather which was passed from teller to teller (and to the rappers, fiddlers, ballad singers, and operatic sopranos who joined us); a small gamelan chime to accompany some of the improvisations; and Granny — a one-foot-high old woman with a red shawl who sat in a tiny white rocking chair and offered wise commentary in a Yiddish accent.

The audience varied from week to week, though many people came to all seven evenings. During "The Book of the Dead" there was storytelling, praise singing, music, rap, riddles, dream talk, discussion. Sometimes a traditional story would come to mind, and somebody would tell it. We spent very little time speculating about the psychology of either the father or son. The young, unfortunately, find many reasons to kill themselves these days. His story can be found every day in the papers or the late-night news. But the father's act transforms the story into a Greek tragedy. The ancient plays said little about the moods or personalities of their doomed protagonists. Their deeds invite our notice but resist our interpretation. I don't even remember the names I'd read in the original newspaper article, though "Rosedale bridge" stayed with me. Rosedale is a nice part of town, and that detail made me imagine this as a middle-class tragedy.

I had never improvised a story before, let alone one that ran for seven weeks. Each evening formed a "chapter" of this spoken-aloud book, and I often felt stretched to the very limit of my imagination and spontaneity as we searched for the right word, the right image to add to the evening. One night, for example, I said, "You never commit suicide in your dreams." I haven't studied psychology to verify this notion, but it feels true to me. A dream lets you turn self-hate into an external monster, a bad guy with a knife who chases you up a dead-end alley. Whatever oppresses you can, in a dream, be embodied as a vicious ogre. The topic of that chapter became: What does a young man dream about on the night before he kills himself? It was the last moment when he was open to life, open to a new story. We made up the dreams he might have had that night.

On another night, Granny spoke up. She said, rather cryptically, "You're always saying, 'They jumped to their death.' So what about 'jumping to your life' for a change?" My puppet spoke wisdom, but what did it mean? How do we jump to our life? By skipping, of course! You could certainly jump to your death from subway platform or bridge, but nobody in the history of the world has ever skipped to their death! So I asked people to think of all the skipping rhymes they could remember.

Celia Lottridge (a well-known storyteller and writer) recalled this one:

Little Minnie Ha-Ha
Went to see her papa
Papa died, Minnie cried
Minnie had a baby, and she called him Tiny Tim
She put him in a bathtub to teach him how to swim
He drank up all the water
And he ate up all the soap
And he died last night with a bubble in his throat
In came the doctor
In came the nurse
In came the lady with the alligator purse
"Mumps," said the doctor
"Measles," said the nurse
"Dead," said the lady with the alligator purse

This rhyme launched a three-week story about the life
and times of Minnie Ha-Ha, a woman who never lost her
ability to laugh. We imagined Minnie as a woman who'd
led a rough, thoroughly modern life (including losing a son
during the war). She was a survivor, and her wisdom and
humour were antidotes to suicide. On the seventh night,
Minnie's fictional life dovetailed with what we had imagined of the Torontonian father and son. They had stopped
hearing their own mini "ha-ha," the inner voice of their
own ongoing story, the skipping rhythm of heart and feet
that gives us the courage to continue.

To end "The Toronto Book of the Dead" we remembered aloud why we'd come together in the first

place. All of our stories, poems, praise songs, raps were an offering in memory of two souls who had died in our city. The son had jumped because he had run out of stories. The father died because he had run out of sons. The storytellers of the city have remembered them.

JANE AND THE GARGOYLE

Whenever I walk by our neighbourhood gargoyle, I think of Jane Jacobs. I live in the unnameable Toronto neighbourhood around Vaughan Road and St. Clair Avenue West. Unlike many areas of the city, ours stubbornly resists adjectives and nicknames. We're not cool like Queen Street West, or socially advanced like the Annex, or California-ish like the Beach. We tend to mock the real estate agents' well-intentioned efforts to call us "Hillcrest," "Wychwood Heights," or, as one office building so infelicitously has it, "Clairhurst." The best designation I've ever heard came from my son, seven years old at the time, when we were walking along St. Clair. "Dad," he said, "you know how people talk about Little Italy and Chinatown and Little India ... well, we live in Worldtown."

He was right. If you stroll a few blocks west from Vaughan along St. Clair, you'll notice cafés serving Chinese, Italian, Korean, Greek, Filipino, Middle Eastern, Turkish, Ecuadorian, Cuban, Mexican, Peruvian, Colombian, Thai, Jamaican, Portuguese, Spanish, and Dutch food. We also have two French patisseries and Ellington's, a café where the poets, filmmakers, musicians, and storytellers of the *quartier* like to congregate. Worldtown, indeed.

We also have our own gargoyle. It perches on the lintel at the bank on the southwest corner of Vaughan and St. Clair, probably left there by a construction worker with a sense of humour. This freestanding gargoyle is the size of a small cat, with swept-back wings and outsize talons. It looks out over the intersection with a fierce grimace, stone talons gripping the ledge, casting its gaze on the street scene below and no doubt scaring the shit out of the local pigeons. Few people even know it's there, even though they walk under it every day of their lives. Like most Torontonians, they keep their eyes focussed on the goal ahead, and their feet moving firmly towards it. We tend to stride more than we stroll, and little, local gargoyles are best noticed by dawdlers and *flâneurs,* those who take the time to look up, down, and sideways, and not only straight ahead.

I like to think that the whole neighbourhood, whether or not we know about the secret – though perfectly visible – gargoyle in our midst, benefits from its protection. In medieval society, they would build gargoyles into church walls, partly to make their waterspouts more interesting, but mostly to invoke a kind of reverse protective magic for the townspeople. They wanted to out-ugly the devil himself. The more ferocious the ornament, the better able it would be to repel the myriad forms of bad luck that can assail a community.

Our gargoyle almost had a companion from the

realm of myth. A master Inuit sculptor living at the Native Men's Residence on Vaughan decided to make a mask that would stand on an inukshuk in front of Na-Me-Res. I saw him one evening as he carved, polished, and tenderly rinsed an extravagantly hideous soapstone mask at the corner of Tumivut, a shelter for Native youth (it has a mural that says: "Celebrating 20,000 years of being in the neighbourhood"). I offered the sculptor a small cigar and asked about the mask. After a long, thoughtful pause, he uttered one word: "Spirit." I waited. The story was elaborated: "From up north." Then, ten minutes later: "Keeps bad things away." Unfortunately, just after it was mounted, an inebriated passerby knocked the mask to the ground. Not long after, the sculptor got carried away by his own demons. I heard he pawned his carving tools, and, before he died, we used to see this immensely gifted artist panhandling at Bloor and Spadina.

It seems particularly apt that my part of Toronto has a gargoyle. Vaughan and St. Clair is undoubtedly the most medieval corner of the city. The high and low and in-between of society mix here the way they must have in a fourteenth-century marketplace. Beggars in front of Shoppers Drug Mart share the sidewalk with the rich parking their Jaguars. Albert Wiggan, of Albert's Real Jamaican Foods (a "neighbourhood public figure," to use Jane Jacobs's phrase), offers street-corner philosophy to all who need it (and even those who don't). He is our version of Harry Bailly, Chaucer's Keeper of the Tabard Inn, who encourages the pilgrims to share their tales on the high road to Canterbury. Sacred and secular commingle as monks from the Zen temple get toasted coconut ice cream from Dutch Dreams, or Filipina nuns from the Catholic church wait for the streetcar. When our youngest son was aged three, he once stood at the corner of Vaughan and St. Clair and beheld a workman wearing a hard hat and a belt laden with tools. He looked him up and down, and then asked, "What kind of man are you?" The man, not skipping a beat, replied, "What kind of a little boy are you?" It is the kind of city neighbourhood where it somehow makes sense to wonder about what kind of people we all are, what roles in society we fulfill, and what has brought such a motley crew of the world's pilgrims together in this particular urban village. And, just above and slightly angled towards the intersection, our gargoyle surveys it all, a small, stone protector of the St. Clair West commons.

Which brings me, in a meandering, medieval way, back to Jane Jacobs. Like our neighbourhood guardian spirit, Jane Jacobs had a way of perching in the very middle of everyday life, yet high enough above the fray to watch what she called the marvellously subtle and spontaneously choreographed "ballet" of the streets, sidewalks, and citizens. As I walk past our gargoyle, I imagine Jane sharing the perch, observing with fierce and loving eye the dance of the neighbourhood, and listening with Chaucer-like generosity to the many stories of Worldtown.

A FOLK TALE FOR THE CBC

The old story begins like this: Once upon a time, so long ago the good old days were still to come, and nobody carried watches but everybody always had enough time, a hunter was walking along a jungle trail and found a skull. The skull, to his astonishment, said, "Hi." The hunter gasped, "What brought you here?" "Talking brought me here," the skull said, "and by the way, don't tell anyone about me." The hunter promised, hurried on to the village, and said to the chief, "You'll never believe this! There's a skull on a path in the jungle...."

Before I tell you what happens next, let me point out that this is a folk tale, and folk tales are meant to be heard, not read. Joe Neil MacNeil, a great storyteller from Cape Breton, used to say, "What the ear does not hear cannot move the heart." So the best thing would be if we could trade stories directly – you tell me yours, I'll tell you mine. It's called the oral tradition, and it is enjoying a surprising renaissance in Canada and around the world. This is surprising, because storytelling comes out of cultures where people had more time to talk and listen than we do today. In our society, we have countless ways to communicate, but not very much to say. There's a story about that. An anthropologist was apparently in an African village when the first television arrived. For a couple of weeks, the villagers watched TV non-stop. Then they began drifting back to the old storyteller by the fire, until nobody was left watching television. When the anthropologist pointed out that the TV knew so many more stories than the old man, one of the villagers responded, "Yes, the TV knows more stories, but the storyteller knows me." This may explain why, a few years ago, after I told a forty-five minute folk tale to a gym full of so-called "at-risk" teenagers (school staff surrounded the audience in case a riot broke out), one of the boys came up – a six-footer with cap turned backwards, and pants sagging over his basketball shoes – and said, "Yo, sir, that story was better than Nintendo...." I took it as a tribute not to my performance abilities but to the power of the oral tradition, still alive and well and able to hold teens in a reverie in the early twenty-first century.

By the way, it's not surprising that teenagers love folk tales. As the African novelist Chinua Achebe said, "Storytellers threaten all champions of control." Folk tales specialize in mocking the pretentious and the powerful. They favour those who live with courage and open-hearted spontaneity. Their protagonists are always "at risk." And the greatest thing about folk tales, perhaps especially for teenagers, is that they counsel us to pay attention to the unlikeliest voices: a dusty mouse, a dishevelled beggar, a dream – or even a talking skull. In old-time stories, the true hero is the one who breaks their journey to listen to the raggedy creature by the side of the road, the creature who says, "Traveller, share your bread, and I will share my wisdom." Teens feel the truth of this moral stance keenly, for they themselves are the unregarded voices of the adult world.

Although this cultural phenomenon has mostly flourished off the media's radar, radio is a natural home for storytelling. My friend Itah Sadu and I recently pitched a storytelling show to the CBC. Itah is an African-Canadian storyteller and writer. My own background is Jewish, Romanian, Turkish, French, and American. We're a true crossroads duo, and, perhaps because of that, we both love oral stories, from street stories to family history to the old folk tales. Wanting to expand the age and cultural bandwidth of the CBC, we proposed a show that would explore how and why Canadians tell each other stories. But the pilot episode for *Big Mouth* (our decidedly un-Canadian title) included two folk tales, and that, according to the new program development committee, was our downfall. The rejection letter stated, "There is no interest in traditional stories told in traditional ways at this time." The letter went on to say they only want shows that will appeal to an "urban" audience, shows with an "edge." As for the story of the talking skull, which Itah told on the pilot, the CBC's comment was that their longed-for demographic (young, urban, multicultural) would only be interested in a story like this if it took place in an alleyway off Yonge Street, not "on a jungle path somewhere."

But is that true? Do all of you culturally diverse, twenty-to-thirty-year-old city dwellers only like stories about stuff you see on your own streets and sidewalks? What about stories that take place in worlds we travel to via our imaginations? Besides, the distance between "some jungle path somewhere" and a big city alleyway isn't so great after all. Boonaa Mohammed, a brilliant, young spoken word poet we interviewed for our pilot, grew up hearing folk tales from his parents, who were political refugees from the Horn of Africa. Now he spins his contemporary stories at spoken word slams. He grew up speaking "Story," and it informs his work as a contemporary poet. That's the point. Folk tales are a vocabulary of the imagination. They enable us to speak about things that are almost beyond the power of words to express, whether they take place in alleyways or jungle paths.

Which brings me back to our mysterious and talkative skull. In the traditional version, the hunter, of course, can't keep his secret, and brings the chief back to the skull. "Talk, skull!" he says. But the skull stays silent. The chief is not amused, and the guard's sword flashes. As the hunter's head rolls towards the skull, the skull says, "You see, my unfortunate and big-mouthed friend, talking brought me here, and talking brought you here, too." A comment on our very human inability to keep juicy secrets? As the Jamaicans say, "Mouth open, story jump out!" Or does the story remind us not only to listen for strange voices along the way but also to pay close attention to what they say? That's the way with folk tales – they raise questions more than providing a final say. That's why they're so truly edgy, and why my gym full of teenagers sat so still for so long.

But the CBC has a point. Folk tales change, get updated, grow; the oral tradition is a living tapestry of old patterns rewoven with new yarn. A Tuscan proverb says: A story is not delicious unless you add your own spice. So here's "The Talking Skull" remix, for the CBC.

A freelance radio producer was walking by an alleyway behind the CBC building in Toronto, and found a skull. The skull, to his astonishment, began speaking to him: "Pitching brought me here. I pitched a show about storytelling in Canada to the CBC, and this is what happened. If you're going in there, you'd better not mention me. Seriously, don't say a word – or else." The freelancer promised, hurried into the building, and found the committee for new program development. "I want to pitch an amazing new show!" he said. He was thinking, what could be cooler, edgier, and more urban than a storyteller's skull in a downtown alley? But should he pitch it or should he keep his promise? What's the worst that could happen if he told?

I can't tell you what happened next because the story is still in progress. We don't know if our skulls will wind up out there in the alley. If you tune in to the radio and hear a folk tale, you'll know the managers have changed their minds and put away their swords. But if you're passing by that alleyway and see more than one skull, you'll know how this story ended. Stay tuned. And even if you don't hear any – or enough – stories on the CBC, you can always, in true oral tradition fashion, swap some with your neighbours.

THE MAYOR AND THE STORYTELLER

Stories capture more votes than policies, and the strongest metaphor wins the election. Humans are story-tropic creatures: We like suspense, and we're drawn to tales of heroes, quests, and courage, even in politics. The right understands this better than the left these days. We saw, south of the border, how the positive rallying cry of "yes we can!" lasted about two years before the "Tea Party" – a perennially evocative trope in American politics – kicked its metaphoric butt. President Obama, a master storyteller before his election, lost his narrative mojo as the Republicans found a vocabulary that, true or not, was more emotionally vivid. George Lakoff, author of *Moral Politics*, rather wistfully pointed out in a blog last winter that it would be good to "loosen the conservative grip on public discourse." Stories enrich our expressive vocabulary and give us new ways to imagine and talk about social and political change.

Aesop knew this well. In one of his more subversive fables, Lion, Fox, and Donkey go hunting. Lion asks Donkey to divide the meat, and Donkey divides it into three equal parts. Then Lion kills him, tosses the carcass on the pile, and asks Fox to try. Fox pushes everything over to Lion except for one dead crow. "How did you learn to divide things so equally?" Lion asks. "I studied with the dead donkey," replies Fox. A useful, if chilling, story to remember in the age of Enron, Lehman Brothers, and the widening gap between the rich and the rest of us.

Stories, of course, can work their persuasive magic for all sides of a debate, and we saw this phenomenon at work in 2010 in two municipal elections in Canada. Progressive Calgary mayor Naheed Nenshi told his election-winning story through a multimedia series of twelve Better Ideas, where he described Calgary as a great city that can and will be even greater: "Calgary will be a city where its citizens are enriched by outstanding libraries, recreation amenities, and a vibrant cultural scene; Calgary will be a city where every neighbourhood is a safe neighbourhood; Calgary will be a city that reduces the number of people living in poverty and ensures opportunity for all." Nenshi's telling of what Calgary *will be* was not only an effective way to make his listeners want to know what happens next; it also assured them they have the power to make this visionary story come true. While he was telling his stirring narrative in Calgary, we were hearing a very different kind of story here in Toronto, from a very different – though equally compelling – yarnspinner.

I'm a professional storyteller, and when Rob Ford

ran for mayor last fall, I felt a secret, collegial pride that he used the art of storytelling to beat his narratively challenged opponents. Although I didn't like his story much, I had to agree that Mr. Ford told the strongest tale, and he was duly rewarded by winning the election. There are, of course, differences between Mr. Ford's storytelling practice and mine. When I tell folk tales, I don't have to persuade my listeners to do anything but enjoy and remember the stories. My stories don't have to ridicule opposing opinions, or convince my audience that I know how to eradicate their deficits, or win me power over anything except boredom. One day I was telling once-upon-a-time stories to a group of grade two kids. When I said the show was almost over, one little boy piped up: *"Never* finish!" I took it as a compliment because boring stories, like, for example, your neighbours' home videos, make us want to shout: "Finish *now!"* With good stories, you enjoy the suspense as you wait to hear what happens next.

After that same show, another child asked me, with a seven-year-old's unabashable honesty: "Sir, are all storytellers professional liars, or just some of them?" I don't remember what I told him, but what I wish I'd said was: Storytellers use fiction to tell the truth, and the more stories you know, the more ways you have to tell the truth. And the more truth you know, the more courage you have to make a difference in the world.

I wish I'd also warned my little boy about storytellers you shouldn't trust, the ones who use fiction not to lead you towards the truth but away from it. As the Jewish saying goes, "He's such a liar that not only what he says isn't true, even the *opposite* of what he says isn't true." Which brings me to His Worship Mayor Rob Ford.

Whether or not you agree with his political views, it's true that Mr. Ford told us a classic and compelling story; we've watched versions of it in countless westerns, and it works every time. An outsider rides into a town to bring justice to its oppressed citizens. In his version, Mr. Ford (and what a *great* name for a maverick lawman!) comes riding in from the suburbs in a badly fitting suit (storytelling rule: the more awkward the outsider looks, the better for the narrative) to free the town from the unjust rule of a powerful clique.

In Mr. Ford's story, our municipal leaders were, through malice and/or sheer incompetence, frivolously wasting our hard-earned tax dollars. City Council presided over a veritable Niagara Falls of misspent money, or worse: a backroomers' paradise where insiders got rewarded with juicy taxpayer-funded benefits. However questionable the details, Mr. Ford told his story convincingly and well. It had a plausible outsider hero, a quest, a dash of suspense, and, most importantly, a memorable punchline. By the end of the campaign, Ford didn't even have to tell the whole thing. With two code words – *gravy train* – he could conjure the whole, irresistible story, and it made him the most powerful mayor in Canada. Stories truly do win elections.

But as a Caribbean friend of mine likes to say, "The

leaky roof can fool the sun, but it can't fool the rain." Our mayor's original tale, about being a renegade hero come to rescue us from self-serving and inept politicians, has sprung many leaks. It has morphed into a narrative we *didn't* vote for. The inscription on Eldon Garnet's sculpture on the Queen Street bridge states: *this river I step in is not the river I stand in.* In our mayor's case, the story we stepped in is definitely not the story we're standing in now. We storytellers may be "professional liars," as my grade-two friend said, but we do have our principles, and one of them is that you can't switch stories midstream.

There were signs of narrative trouble early in Rob Ford's mayoral reign. One of his first acts in office was cancelling the vehicle registration tax, then complaining that the city didn't have enough revenue to cover its costs. The Irish call this "putting on the poor mouth," i.e., pretending to be poorer than you really are. Then the mayor's brother, Councillor Doug Ford, began talking about how anything that "wasn't nailed down" would be sold off, privatized, or just plain axed in the name of running a cheaper ship of state. Nailed down? That was a new metaphor indeed, and it became the recurrent motif of Mayor Ford's new story, where elements of a hard-earned and long-established common good – libraries, parks, arts programs, police, firefighters, support for our youth – weren't "nailed down" sufficiently to be safe from the impending cuts. Writing about how conservatives in the U.S. have hijacked the vocabulary that describes a government's duty of care to its citizens, George Lakoff writes, "Services ... start where necessities end. ... It is time to stop speaking of government 'services' and speak instead of government providing necessities" ("Untellable Truths," *Huffington Post* Dec. 10, 2010) How the mayor's recent decision not to accept provincially funded public health nurses fits into any kind of meaningful, city-building story is anybody's guess.

By the time KPMG's due diligence found no evidence of a "gravy train" at City Hall, Mr. Ford had already, with the help of his brother and friends on Council, begun telling us his new story about Toronto becoming the Incredible Shrinking City, where the government will provide fewer and fewer services – or *necessities* – to its citizens. First we listened to a story about "cutting the waste," then we found out that we *are* the waste. Things that many generations of Torontonians had agreed were important and valuable parts of civic life were now being spoken of as disposable assets.

When did our big-hearted maverick hero start shooting up the place instead of saving it?

Mayor Ford's first story has stuttered to a stop, and his new Toronto story is still missing something: the moment of collective revelation when we learn something new and wonderful about what it means to live here at the crossroads of the world. His current tale about dismantling what isn't "nailed down" is hardly a story at all, for all we're waiting to hear about is what we're going to lose next, and where's the suspense in that? I once heard a ten-year-old storyteller at Wilkinson Public School begin her family history by saying, "This is a true and a *strong* story." With due respect, storyteller to storyteller, I'd like to suggest to Mr. Ford that he try telling us a true and a strong story about what our city *can* be, not what it can't.

STORIES WITHOUT BORDERS

A year ago I went to Israel to perform at the Israel Storytelling Festival, and, while there, went to Ramallah to visit a Palestinian friend, a scholar of folklore. We had met in Europe three years before, and I had a standing invitation to come across the border for a coffee. When I mentioned to my Israeli friends and family that I had a friend "over there," they cautioned me against the trip. They were also surprised that I, a Jew, had a Palestinian friend. I pointed out that an invitation was an invitation, that artists don't have as much regard for borders as politicians, and that this particular friend told marvellous stories she'd collected from Palestinian women – stories worth crossing borders to hear.

I took a taxi from Jerusalem, passed through the checkpoint, drove through the bustling and confusing streets of Ramallah, and miraculously found her apartment building. We had strong coffee and ate a delicious lunch with her fourteen-year-old son. I may have been the first Jew her son had met who wasn't wearing a uniform. He loved telling risqué jokes, and I suggested, scandalizing his mother, he consider a career in stand-up. She was hoping for doctor or lawyer (which sounded familiar to my Jewish ears).

Later, we went to a café and, over ice cream, swapped stories of Hodja Nasrudin, the "wise fool" of the Middle East. These wonderfully subversive stories are relished by Jews, Christians, and Muslims. Hodja stories truly cross all frontiers and borders. She told me about the time Hodja was asked to give a speech at the mosque. When he came to speak, unfortunately he forgot the words he had memorized. He said, "My friends, do you know what I've come to speak about?" No, they replied, they didn't. "In that case," said Hodja, "how can I tell you? I'll come back next week." It happened again: He forgot everything, asked the same question, and this time, remembering what had happened the week before, everyone said, "Yes, Hodja, we know!" "Good. Then I don't have to tell you!" He walked away. The third week, like a Toastmaster's worst nightmare, he forgot his speech again. "My friends, how many of you know what I've come to speak about today?" Half of them said, "We know!" and the other half cried, "We don't know!" "That's fine," said Hodja. "Let those who know tell those who don't!" And he never gave that much-promised speech.

Ramallah and Tel Aviv must be the world capitals of *carpe diem*. The media rarely reports the sheer *joie de vivre*, warmth, and extraordinary hospitality that animates both Israeli and Palestinian society. One thing I noticed, however, was that hope was a forbidden topic. After so many years of bitter disappointment, nobody on either side of the wall wanted to imagine or talk about the future.

My first night in Israel I had a dream. In my dream, the negotiations were taking place, but on one condition: nobody could talk. Everything was being negotiated through a board game, a bit like Monopoly. The settlements, refugees, rocket fire, Gilad Schalit, the borders, the blockade, Gaza — all the issues were on the board, and the one rule was that the players had to keep playing silently, without words. It seems that once words were taken out of the game, the players could concentrate on the real issues, and, by the end of the game, everything had been resolved and peace had been achieved. When I related my dream it provoked rueful laughter. Most of my Israeli friends said they didn't care if the Palestinians ever said the words "Israel is a Jewish state." They just wanted an end to violence. And I suspect my Palestinian friend had stopped caring about the words of politicians a long time ago. She just wanted her son to live without checkpoints and walls.

I reminded her that all the walls of human history eventually fall out of fashion or use. We spoke about Berlin and about the heavily policed border that once separated north and south in Ireland. It will certainly be that this wall also becomes unnecessary, although probably not for a few generations. I had a storyteller's fantasy about the wall while I was there. (The purpose of storytellers is to give voice to the possible in the midst of impossibilities.) One day the Israelis and Palestinians could take all of those mighty slabs of concrete, pile them up on whatever border they finally agree to, cover their new mountain with trees, and name it Mt. Used-to-be-a-Wall. People would make pilgrimages from around the world to stand at the top, look in all directions, and say to each other: "Did you know that this used to be a wall?" Talk about a boost for tourism! What a joy it would be to stand on *that* mountain!

Before leaving the café I told my friend a story that was told to me by an Israeli storyteller who heard it from an Arab friend. (What goes around comes around, even if it goes through a checkpoint to get there!) A man left his land in the care of another man. The other man took good care of it for a long time. The man came back and asked for his land, but the other man said no, he had cared for it for so long and made it so fruitful that the land belonged to him now. They had a quarrel, and they asked the judge to decide the dispute. The judge happened to be Hodja Nasrudin. "The land belongs to me!" one man shouted. "The land belongs to me!" shouted the other. Hodja got down on the ground and put his ear to the earth. "What are you doing?" they asked. "I'm listening," he replied. "What are you listening to?" "The land." "And what does the *land* have to say?" they asked incredulously. Hodja looked up and said, "The land says that *both* of you belong to the land."

I left Ramallah and returned to the storytelling festival. The Israeli storytellers wanted to invite my friend to the festival, but I had to tell them she wasn't ready to cross that particular border. It did occur to me, however, that, if enough stories manage to pass through enough checkpoints, the people on both sides of the wall may one day rekindle their belief in a neighbourly future. Futures, after all, come to pass, whether or not we're able to talk about them ahead of time. Perhaps real wisdom will come, like in my friend's Hodja story, not from the sermon the wise fool keeps forgetting, but only when both halves of the assembly start talking directly to each other.

STORYTELLERS' GAME: A MYTH REMIX

"Go on listening, carefully, respectfully. After a while the earth feels free to speak."
—Mario Vargas Llosa, *The Storyteller*

"Ten"

"Listener was going along ..."

The game might begin something like that. In our storytelling game, we'll be making believe that we are modern mythtellers. We'll also pretend that our new myth features a mysterious force called Listener. We could call our game: Let's tell a myth in the early twenty-first century. Or: Let's try telling each other mysterious, useful, memorable stories about the power of listening and imagine they are parts of a long, interconnected narrative. Or we could just start playing and figure out what to call the whole thing later.

"Our modern alienation from myth is unprecedented," grimly warns Karen Armstrong in *A Short History of Myth*. This means that, even if we want to learn how to be mythtellers, we don't really know the rules of the game, or what needs to happen next, or where the whole thing will wind up. And I should probably admit right away that I've never played this game myself, though I would passionately like to learn how. Sometimes it seems like my entire training and life as a contemporary storyteller has brought me to the very edge of what could be, once we start, an exhilarating, timely, even necessary game. But perhaps counting down to the game's launch is the best we can do for now. "With myths," Italo Calvino suggests in *Six Memos for the Next Millennium*, "one should not be in a hurry." Myth, like all oral narrative, is slow literature.

"Nine"

Discovering how Listener could be the heart and hero of a new myth, and why such a myth may be worth learning and telling in today's world, will take us, via a meandering route, to the very edge of our storytelling knowledge and beyond. This is, after all, a new game, and, although mythtelling has certainly thrived for long stretches of human history, we have little evidence of societies recasting themselves as mythkeeping cultures. We've chronicled many instances of the erosion of myth and oral tradition, but we've rarely imagined how a culture could move towards myth, or how storytellers could reinvent themselves as mythtellers. Our literary and anthropological accounts note the death and dying of mythtelling but not its potential for rediscovery. Our game, when we start playing it, will lead us into new and unprecedented cultural territory.

Later on, I'll exercise dealer's choice and propose that in our mythtelling game we agree to tell stories about listening, and in particular the possibility of listening to voices that speak from beyond our customary bandwidth of perception. We'll gather episodes of Listener, the myth hero of our myth-to-be, from around a summer camp campfire, from traditional fairy tales, by a crib in the neonatal intensive care unit, on the banks of the Yukon River, and in myriad moments in life and literature. And, as we collect these examples of listening, we'll imagine that they form part of a myth—that is, that they are part of a cycle of mysterious, long, interconnected, useful stories that speak about extreme and necessary experiences in human and beyond-human life, stories that are meant to be told by word of mouth.

Speaking of telling, there is a large body of writing that describes myth, both ancient and "new," in terms of psychology, planetary health, social justice, mysticism, ecological awareness, political change, and so on. In most of these contemporary studies, treatises, and manifestos, the orality of myth is missing in action. Myth is understood, in these accounts, as something distant, inert, an object of study that stays safely remote in its own world rather than demanding a life-changing presence in ours. Yet, if the word of mouth quality of myth means anything, it must mean that myth is always in transit from a teller to a listener, who will become the next teller, and so on. Myth is always in need of a voice, a listener, an occasion in which to be given utterance. Although we paradoxically meet myth mostly in written form, myth is a form of oral narrative, meant to be spoken aloud from teller to listener within communities that prize their disciplined ability to remember such stories for immensely long periods of history.

So myths are for telling, and our new myth – assuming we can learn to play the role of mythtellers – will have to speak to us, first of all, through our own voices. The counsel of an oral story, writes Walter Benjamin in *Illuminations*, is not revealed as the answer to a question, but rather as "a proposal concerning the continuation of a story which is just unfolding. To seek this counsel, one would first have to be able to tell the story." So now, by acknowledging myth's spoken-aloud force and form, we are upping the ante. In our new myth, not only will Listener be going along, launching, blessing, animating, and teaching us to embody an extraordinary quality of listening, but these remarkable, mythic adventures of listening will have to be worthy of oral narration.

But before Listener can go along, let's consider the challenges of playing this particular game.

"Eight"

There are many challenges involved in playing the game, even before we begin. For one thing, even if we could figure out how to play the role of mythtellers, we don't really know what kinds of myth we can or should be telling today. Karen Armstrong proposes, idealistically, that our story-impoverished world needs "myth that will help us to identify with all our fellow-beings, not simply with those who belong to our ethnic, national, or ideological tribe. We need myths that help us to realize the importance of compassion, which is not always regarded as sufficiently productive or efficient in our pragmatic, rational world. We need myths that help us to create a spiritual attitude, to see beyond our immediate requirements, and enable us to experience a transcendent value that challenges our solipsistic selfishness. We need myths that help us to venerate the earth as sacred once again instead of merely using it as a 'resource.' This is crucial, because unless there is some kind of spiritual revolution that is able to keep abreast of our technological genius, we will not save our planet" (*A Short History of Myth*). This is a fairly grand, world-mending order, especially if you consider that, by her own account, we don't live in an age that knows much about myth, mythtelling, and mythlistening. How, one may well wonder, can we invent such an ambitious myth nowadays, however desperate we may be for its world-transforming benefits?

I respect and am moved by Armstrong's inspiring *cri de coeur*, but our goal here is more modest. We'll be approaching myth as game players, not scholars, definers, explainers, or even visionaries. Our self-assigned task isn't to study and report on mythtelling as a literary, cultural, or spiritual practice or artifact, or as the verbal element of an exotic ritual from a faraway time and place. We don't have to observe or speculate about what a new myth could or should do and be. We simply have to play a mythtelling game we've never played before.

And speaking of challenges, I suspect we'd all agree with Armstrong that we (we: modern, urban, industrial, computerized folk) live in a world that feels impossibly distant from the kinds of oral cultures where myth is told, heard, and lived by. "Because a people coevolve with their habitat," writes Sean Kane in *Wisdom of the Mythtellers*, "because they walk the paths their ancestors walked, mythtelling assumes that the stories already exist in nature, waiting to be overheard by humans who will listen for them." He is writing about hunting/gathering societies quite remote from our age, marked as it is by a vast disconnect from the idea that nature holds necessary wisdoms, and that our ancestors once believed it was good to overhear and partake in those deeply rooted stories.

This divide is real. We know there have been many places and times and societies where mythtelling was an essential part of intellectual, spiritual, and practical life, but I doubt anyone today would argue that we inhabit one of those myth-loving ages. Unless we happen to be born and raised in one of the world's few remaining oral cultures, we have surprisingly few clues as to what mythtellers and myth listeners (their essential companions) do, feel, believe, or how they sustain themselves from one generation to the next. In a society where we double-click our way through endless data hoards, we can barely imagine what it might mean to carry your culture in your head, knowing that the most thrilling and essential information, distilled into long, inter-connected, mysterious, suspenseful, useful, memorable, word of mouth narratives that talk about extreme and necessary things in human and beyond-human life, is always one disciplined, attentive listener away from disappearing. In our world, not only do we not walk ancestral paths, we've almost forgotten what it means to have ancestors in the first place.

"Seven"

Another thing that marks our distance from myth, even as it adds to its romance, is the fact, noted earlier, that myth lives by word of mouth. Myth thrives in cultures that prize the spoken word, that celebrate on a daily basis the ability to use language precisely, musically, and memorably. This means that myth narratives are wonderfully portable and adapted for use on a daily basis. Oral stories, especially the important ones (and myths are perhaps the most important stories humans have created), are meant to travel with you as you go through everyday life. In Chinua Achebe's book *Anthills of the Savannah*, an elder gives an eloquent speech, rallying his fellow villagers to an effort of resistance against the reigning dictator. As he reminds them to live by the values of their traditional stories, he says, "The story is our escort. Without it, we are blind. Does the blind man own his escort? No, neither do we the story; rather it is the story that owns and directs us." In this description, stories are navigational tools of unequalled power, maps that serve to guide us on what poet Robert Bringhurst calls "the paths between the worlds ... The paths, for instance, between the world of the village and the world of the forest; between childhood and marriage, community and solitude, and the paths between the worlds of life and death, and the worlds of waking and dreaming". (from his introduction to Alice Kane's *Dreamer Awakes*). Of all the genres of oral storytelling, myth, in speaking of cosmic doings, may be the narrative form designed to interweave most deeply and intimately with the adventures and routines of everyday life.

The late Angela Sidney, an elder from Tagish, Yukon, was one of the few mythtellers I knew personally. She came to the Fifth Toronto Storytelling Festival in 1983, and I had several opportunities to see her in the Yukon in the years before her death. Mrs. Sidney knew a traditional story for every river and mountain in her homeland. She knew the family and tribal genealogies for many generations. She truly walked in the paths of her ancestors, in Kane's telling phrase. Myth was so comprehensively interwoven with her life that when anthropologist Julie Cruikshank asked her to recount facts from her life – for example, what it was like when they built the Alaska Highway – she would begin her answer by telling a myth. "From the beginning," Cruikshank writes, "several of the eldest women responded to my questions about secular events by telling traditional stories.... Each explained that these narratives were important to record as part of her life story" (*Life Lived Like a Story*). Their life experiences were inseparable from the myths they had inherited, kept alive, and called on every day as a source of meaning.

I saw for myself how this could work when I visited Angela Sidney in Whitehorse, Yukon. I used to sit with her by the bank of the Yukon River and listen as she told stories about how Crow made the world. Crow, in her tradition, is a cosmic shoplifter, a trickster who subverts every attempt to hoard the essentials of civilized and planetary life. For example, when a sea lion chief tries to keep all the land to himself on his own private island, back when the world was covered with water, Crow tricks him into releasing some of it into Crow's supremely generous care. Crow throws the sand out on the water and some of it floats. Then he calls out, "Become a world!" The sand turns into the earth, and Crow welcomes all creatures to tread, run, crawl, and walk upon it.

While she told me her creation tales, I'd sometimes notice a real crow – black, impertinent, curious – hopping around on the grass by the river, and I would wonder why Angela Sidney's people had named the creator after a bird they beheld every day going about its devious, scavenging business. When I saw a crow hopping into earshot of the creation myth it starred in, I'd wonder if my mythtelling friend – and her Tagish and Tlingit ancestors – look at the crow and see Crow, Bringer of Light and Transformer of Worlds. Is that crow-on-the-riverbank also and at the same time the divine and cosmic Crow? And what would it be like to live in a world shoplifted and brought forth into glorious existence by a cosmic force named after a canny, unpredictable, and ever-resourceful bird, one you saw every day pecking alertly through the grass of everyday life?

Even though this intimate relationship to oral myth seems very distant from our own age, there's something immensely attractive about living in a world where stories could matter so much that they can be our escort as we traverse and find meaning in both mundane and extreme experiences. Myth, even to people like me who encounter it mainly in books or scholarly study, has an irresistible allure. Even here, even now, we are drawn to myth like dowsers to a secret spring. At the most fundamental level, it explains why children are so eager to hear their life told back to them at bedtime. They love to hear the stories of their own lives, including the creation myth of how they were born. Then, at around age nine or ten, a sense of the antiquity and, paradoxically, the immediacy of myth takes hold of the imagination.

When I was that age, I fell headlong into the world of gods and goddesses, Greek, Roman, and Norse. Grey-eyed Athena was my favourite, but I also felt a kinship with Apollo and Hermes. Aphrodite was a bit intimidating. What I liked was the sense that these powerful beings once shared the earth with us, that they once shapeshifted their way into our lives, that human beings once lived next door to mystery. Robert

Bringhurst, in his study of Haida mythtellers *A Story As Sharp As a Knife*, writes, "To those who think the myths, the creatures who inhabit them are real and not fictitious." At that age, I thought of Athena with all the passion of a solitary, shy, ten-year-old kid growing up in the Jewish suburbs of Detroit. I also thought, rather ruefully, that it was unlikely I'd ever meet this magnificent, wise, Zeus-sprung goddess in my middle-class neighbourhood near 8 Mile Road. I then went directly from an infatuation with the ancient gods to the more modern semi-divinity known as 007, who, like Zeus, had a predilection for earthly women, whose chariot was an Aston Martin, and whose nectar was a martini, shaken, not stirred.

Myself, I was shaken and stirred by these early encounters with myth, even in their literary form. Alan Garner, in his magnificent novella *The Stone Book*, describes a moment when a child touches the myth world. One day her father, a stonemason, shows Mary a secret passageway to a cave that generations of his people have known about. It is an initiation, and she goes to the cave only when she's old enough to have the courage to enter but is still young enough to fit in the narrow passageway. When she lights her stub of a candle, she sees paintings on the walls around her, paintings of animals, including a bull being killed by an arrow like mark. These are, although she doesn't know it, neolithic paintings thousands of years old. She recognizes the mark as the same one her father uses for his stonemason's mark. Then she looks down and is amazed to see thousands of footprints:

> They are the footprints of people, bare and shod. There were boots and shoes and clogs, heels, toes, shallow ones and deep ones, clear and sharp as if made altogether, trampling each other, hundreds pressed in the clay where only a dozen could stand. Mary was in a crowd that could never have been, thronging, as real as she was. Her feet made prints no fresher than theirs. And the bull was still dying under the mark, and the one hand still held.

When she comes back out, her father says, "That's put a quietness on you." There is a reverent thrill as the window of time opens and the past and present cross-pollinate each other.

And still back with the Greeks, here are Socrates and Phaedrus recollecting a myth as they stroll outside of Athens:

> Phaedrus: Tell me, Socrates, isn't it somewhere about here that they say Boreus seized Orithyia from the river?
> Socrates: Yes, that is the story.

When Phaedrus asks him if he thinks the myth is true, Socrates refuses to measure the story by the standard of scientific fact. Instead, he says, "I can't, as yet, 'know myself,' as the inscription at Delphi enjoins, and so long as that ignorance remains it seems to me ridiculous to inquire into extraneous matters. Consequently, I don't bother about such things, but accept the current beliefs about them, and direct my inquiries, as I have just said, rather to myself, to discover whether I really am a more complex creature and more puffed up with pride than Typhon, or a simpler, gentler being whom heaven has blessed with a quiet, un-Typhonic nature" (*The Collected Dialogues of Plato*, ed. E. Hamilton, H. Cairns). Myth is, in Socrates's description, a frame and force field for understanding his place in the world.

Oral myths are marvellously designed to travel with you, connecting everyday existence with powers, values, and understandings beyond our conventional range of perception, and thus serving as the escorts that Achebe's elder invokes. In another literary example, in J.D. Salinger's story "The Laughing Man" (*Nine Stories*), a gifted camp counsellor tells his tribe of high-spirited nine-year-old New York boys a daily episode from a saga about a hideously deformed, miraculously good-hearted criminal mastermind known as the Laughing Man. The "Comanches" would gather at the front of the bus and listen eagerly to each new installment of "The Laughing Man".... The story infiltrates and guides the lives of these boys. The Laughing Man – a great myth spirit – becomes their courage-bringing escort through the streets, parks, and apartment buildings of New York City.

In *The Lord of the Rings*, a skeptical rider questions Aragorn about the existence of hobbits – "Halflings," laughed the rider ... "Halflings! But they are only a little people in old songs and children's tales out of the North. Do we walk in legends or on the green earth in the daylight?" Aragorn replies, "A man may do both ... for not we but those who come after will make the legends of our time. The green earth, say you? That is a mighty matter of legend, though you tread it under the light of day." Although we operate on different parts of the myth-loving spectrum, for Angela Sidney in Yukon, Socrates on his stroll near Athens, Mary in her Stone Age cave, the young and ardent New Yorkers, an Athena-loving Jewish boy growing up in Detroit, and in Tolkien's imaginary world, myth runs a close parallel to the travails and dilemmas of daily life. That crow on the riverbank really is Crow. The green earth, in all of these real and fictional accounts, is illuminated and made most real by the light of myth.

"Six"

Whether we agree that we live in an unpropitious time for mythtelling, at least let me claim that even nowadays we haven't lost our instinct and hunger for oral stories. Humans are deeply story-tropic creatures, seeking meaning in word of mouth narrative the way sunflowers bend towards the light. We're born ready to hear the voice of the mythteller. We know that the most urgent and interesting wisdom will come from unexpected sources.

"Five"

Robert Bringhurst, in his introduction to Alice Kane's book *The Dreamer Awakes*, uses a biological analogy to describe how oral traditions are sustained by and through storytellers: "[Stories] nest in us as saw-whet owls and wood ducks nest in trees ... [T]hey use us to reproduce themselves." In his account, stories lead a kind of independent yet wholly symbiotic relationship with us, their human hosts. As they are reanimated in and through our voices, they reciprocate our commitment by providing us a moral and imaginary frame for everyday life. He continues, "Stories are not copied; they are reborn, and each succeeding individual is different, yet the species, for long stretches, is substantively the same."

I saw this for myself when I was giving a storytelling workshop for counsellors at Camp Couchiching, on the shores of Lake Couchiching in Ontario. I asked if there was a camp ghost, and the counsellors told me they didn't like telling the kids scary stories, so they had made up a character named Finnigan the Elf. Finnigan was a small creature who helped lost and lonely children. What they didn't realize was that Camp Couchiching is in Anishinabe territory, land that has been continuously inhabited for many thousands of years. When I heard about Finnigan the Elf, I remembered Basil Johnston's story "The Little Boy in the Tree" (from *Next Teller: A Book of Canadian Storytelling*). Johnston, a great Anishinabe storyteller and scholar, describes the *maemaegawaehnse*. They are "a little being akin to an elf, who dwells in the forest. This being bears a special kinship to children, coming to them to uplift their spirits should they be despondent, or conducting them back home should they wander away into the forest on their own." The *maemaegawaehnse* were still alive in the forest by Lake Couchiching. This ancient myth spirit had, in Bringhurst's phrase, simply been "reborn" with a new name.

Even though I suggested earlier that this will be a new game, perhaps our capacity to tell and listen to myth is not so much missing in modern life as unawakened; and the myths themselves, the kinds of narrative maps that could serve as our escorts, are also alive, waiting like the *maemaegawaehnse* for the voices and attention that will give them new life. Perhaps Listener will prove to be, not a new myth spirit, but a very ancient one.

"Four"

How do mythtelling cultures consciously preserve these intricate bodies of word of mouth narrative over so many millennia? What quality of listening, almost unimaginable in today's world, lets people carry myth intact and undiminished between generations of tellers and listeners? Unlike storytellers like me, who are trying to reimagine and revive an almost-lost art, traditional storytellers inherit stories that have been carefully sustained over many centuries; they mature as storytellers with a keen sense of responsibility for keeping these stories alive.

I asked Omushkego elder Pennishish (Louis Bird), who was visiting Toronto for our 2009 Toronto Story-telling Festival, how he was able to remember his vast and complex narrative tradition. First, typically for an old-timer, he demurred, saying that the tradition had already eroded considerably before he decided it was necessary for him to become a storyteller. His grandmother, he said, knew many more of the old stories than he does. Then he told me something I found surprising: "When I remember a story, I'm remembering it in the voice of the person who told it to me." By this account, for Pennishish, and perhaps all tradition-bearers, to be a mythteller is first and foremost to be a keeper of voices, holding and reimagining the polyphony of myth-speaking voices that carry the ancient stories of his Omushkego ancestors.

What a striking way of understanding the nature of myth listening: as a kind of sheltering and continual re-animating of storytellers' voices. Pennishish is a keen observer of the vulnerability of his beloved oral tradition in his own village of Peawanuck, on the west coast of Hudson Bay, and in the wider society around him. How, amid the distractions of modern life, the pain of First Nations poverty, and the active suppression of their traditions by church and state, do his people keep hearing the voices of their ancestors? How do they get their grandchildren to spend endless hours listening to an elder when *Hockey Night in Canada* is on television, or they can

- 204 -

get on Facebook even though they live a thousand kilometres from the end of the road? Pennishish knows first-hand and urgently that once we lose the ability to hold and re-hear the voices of our ancestors, we begin losing the legacy of stories their voices carry.

And if Pennishish is indeed able to hear his stories in the voices of those who told them, then they, on the other side of this timeless equation, must have been imagining his profoundly disciplined, dedicated listening as the destination towards which their stories were and are always travelling. The mythtellers from long ago must have been imagining Pennishish, in the early twenty-first century, still tuning to their ancient frequency. They could never, I'm sure, have taken this quality of millennia-long listening for granted. They must have known, as he certainly does as a mythteller in modern society, just how susceptible their word of mouth stories would always be to the depredations of time and forgetfulness.

"Three"

Pennishish is a mythteller by necessity, trained and able to remember and retell an enormously complex oral tradition. With the highest stakes imaginable, he tells his stories to keep his culture from dying. But most of us modern storytellers come to the art out of choice, because we just like doing it, not because we inherited and must defend an oral tradition from oblivion.

So why, at this particular crossroads of human history, would a self-declared tribe of storytellers clear a new space for living voices, human memory, community, and story? We are, nowadays, living through a time of unprecedented and troubling change. Our old and familiar customs are breaking down, but the new moral frame and social structure we urgently need have yet to emerge. We are stepping into the future with less connection to ancestral guidance than any generation before us, and, although we have invented amazing technologies for saving and sending data, we are at risk of forgetting our personal, family, and cultural stories. With our multitude of astonishing communications technologies, it seems that we have less and less to say to each other. And yet, in the very midst of this strange age, in the very shadow of the World Wide Web, the art of storytelling is slowly coming off the endangered species list. A Celtic proverb has it that "Every force evolves a form." What force could be compelling the creation of this contemporary storytelling renaissance? What force is evolving such an unusual and unlikely cultural form?

Today's storytellers have spent the last few decades experimenting with an art few of us grew up with. We've reinvented the forms of this art, building our repertoires, developing audiences and gatherings, learning how to perform oral stories in an entertaining (one hopes) way. In Toronto, for example, we have events like 1001 Friday Nights of Storytelling (the world's longest-running storytelling open mic); MothUP, which was renamed as The

Raconteurs (a satellite version of New York's The Moth, devoted to telling life stories); the Toronto Storytelling Festival; a centre called Storytelling Toronto; the [murmur] project, which explores psycho-geography through local oral history projects; The Tellery (my own story-telling organization); and more. We even have, at our weekly open mic, a talking stick, which, while it feels sacred to those of us who like old storytelling customs, began its career as a humble – though nicely carved – tethering post for Andean goats, bought at a Latin American gift store on Bloor Street. Not so grand in its origins, but made so by its repurposed use at our gathering. Sometimes, as we essay and experiment with these traditional forms, it feels like we're reaching back to a distant past, sometimes like we're ambassadors from a possible future. Either way, we're making it up as we go along. We're reinventing the customs of oral culture one fake talking stick at a time.

We have relearned the forms of oral narration before we knew what kinds of stories we wanted to tell. In fact, describing how we develop our storytelling repertoires, tellers will often say, "Stories find the tellers they need." But what does that mean? How do stories find their way to their host-tellers? The question provides a clue as we prepare to play our mythtelling game. For if it makes sense at the level of individual storytellers, could it also be possible that the whole storytelling movement, this unprecedented revival of an ancient and now avant-garde artform, may have come to life in the service of a new story? Could a new story be the force that is evolving this form? Could there be a new narrative – perhaps even a new, long, interconnected, mysterious, useful, memorable, word of mouth cycle of stories able to speak about extreme and necessary things in human and beyond-human existence – slowly coalescing on the tongues and in the imaginations of today's storytellers? Can we imagine that such a story – or just say it: such a myth – has needed an international storytelling renaissance to become audible, speakable, and real through the myriad voices that make up this nobly improbable, under-the-radar cultural movement?

And if there is a story, ancient and/or new, slowly finding its way into the world, what is it about and who are its heroes? If Coyote/Crow/Weesakachak and all the myth world's tricksters are eternally going along in the stories of the First Nations mythtellers, who or what could be going along in our potentially new myth?

And now I will take a flying leap and suggest that we may be hearing Listener's mythic footsteps approaching our twenty-first century barnyard. But why has this new – or perhaps very old – spirit come calling just at this moment of human history? Who is Listener?

"Two"

I can only answer that question from within my own experience as a storyteller, and I can only answer it by telling you a story. In the summer of 1973 I was working at Bolton Camp, a summer camp for poor children from Toronto. My eight-year-old boys were the original lords of misrule, going wild all during the day. But every night, around the campfire, I witnessed a miraculous transformation. When the counsellors began to spin their ghostly yarns by the fire, my crazy boys turned into the greatest listeners in the world. With a few words spoken into the quiet air in the middle of a night-time forest, the storytellers created an astonishing reverie in the souls and eyes of boys who, all day long, ran around like little maniacs. It dawned on me that the art of storytelling, which I'd only read about in university, had not entirely vanished from the world, and that the story fire was still burning brightly in the woods of Bolton Camp. I was filled with a passionate desire to take my place in the circle of tellers and listeners. I decided I had to become a storyteller, not because I wanted to perform (I've always been terribly shy), but because I wanted to keep reveling in the quality of listening I witnessed around that fire.

But I had a big problem. I didn't know any stories. Lacking an oral tradition to call my own, I began to hunt and gather a patchwork repertoire. There wasn't much systematic research involved. I simply listened with eager and endless appetite to every storyteller I could find, especially the old-timers. I read voraciously: myth, epic, saga, folk tale, creation stories. I invented, experimented, improvised, and tried to reweave the old patterns with new yarn. I became a willing host, as Bringhurst describes, for the story seeds, blown in from all corners of the world's oral traditions, which found my voice, memory, and imagination a congenial place to take root. And, story by story, I found a loosely connected bunch of old and original tales I could take into the world. Or perhaps, as we noted earlier, these stories found me. And here is where my own history, mirroring a common experience for modern storytellers, may hold a clue as we prepare to play our mythtelling game. For, after thirty years of telling my catch-as-catch-can repertoire, it dawned on me that a "red thread" ran through almost all of my stories. The stories I was compelled to tell all had to do with listening. Both in the content of these stories and in my work creating gatherings where people could tell and listen to oral stories, I kept returning to the transformative power of listening I witnessed at the Bolton Camp campfire.

In the folk tales that I tell and retell, there is always a moment when the hero, walking along his or her quest-road, hears a voice that says, "Friend, I'm hungry. Share your bread, and I'll share my wisdom." There on the ground, looking up hopefully, is a skinny mouse. Sometimes it's a beggar, a crone, even a dream. The mouse is talking to you. What do you do next? The once-upon-a-time stories counsel you to break your journey, no matter how urgent. Rest awhile. Share your bread, even if you've little enough as it is. Above all, don't show your surprise that the mouse is talking, or your shock that you understand its words. Those who ride haughtily by, too proud to listen to a dusty mouse, condemn themselves to dreary inconsequence; sometimes they get turned to stone, but mostly their terminal mediocrity is its own punishment. It is always the third son or daughter in fairy tales, so often the unregarded, lazy, attention-deficit-disorder, special-education, every-day-in-the-vice-principal's-office, slow-learning kid (like my Bolton Camp boys!) who proves to be the best listener and the true hero. The hero is the one who is open to hearing new voices, even if they come from a weird mouse, a beggar, a crone, or a dream. According to the old wondertales, when things begin to talk to you, stay and listen. Maybe you'll hear an interesting story; maybe the story will be about you. Wisdom, according to the stories I keep returning to, always speaks in unexpected voices. The trick is learning to listen. But how do these stories about listening become part of a myth cycle about Listener? And how do we become the inventors, keepers, and tellers of that myth?

In *The Lord of the Rings*, Tolkien has a wise, old tree creature recall the way the ancient earth dwellers gained their extraordinary power: "They always wanted to talk to everything, the old Elves did." That, it seems to me, could describe the heart of our new myth; the power to listen, the power to communicate beyond our customary bandwidth of understanding – these elven conversational skills could represent our greatest hope for survival today. Humankind has proven tragically adept at hearing and repeating only our own story, thus closing our ears to new and different voices, new and different stories. It isn't always easy to listen like this. We like our talk to come in familiar voices and from familiar places. After Socrates tells Phaedrus an ancient myth, Phaedrus scoffs: "It is easy for you, Socrates, to make up tales from Egypt or anywhere else you fancy." Socrates responds: "Oh, but the authorities of the temple of Zeus at Dodona, my friend, said that the first prophetic utterances came from an oak tree. In fact the people of those days ... were content in their simplicity to listen to trees or rocks, provided these told the truth." We don't go through daily life listening to mice, children, dreams, oak trees, or, as in Harold Courlander's story "Talk," yams: "Well, at last you're here. You never weeded me, but now you come around with your digging stick. Go away and leave me alone!" The farmer runs away screaming when he hears his indignant yam speak up. In Jaime de Angulo's account of California's Pit River people, a shaman gives this advice: If you want to find power, you must be willing to hear about it from strange sources; go walking alone in the mountains; keep your ears open; sing your best medicine song: "The dragonfly came to me / with news from my home. / I lie in the afternoon / looking toward the hills" (*Indian Tales*). When we keep listening, even to unlikely voices, even the dragonfly can bring news from home.

Myths, I'm convinced, are born from shared dreams, and it may be the world is ready for a great new dreaming. We certainly don't need another authorized version of anything, or another canon of official texts. But, judging from my own experience as a storyteller who found himself gathering and carrying a lifetime's-worth of stories about listening, it may be useful to begin to notice and name and narrate Listener's presence in our lives. We could imagine that Listener is present whenever parents tell fairy tales at a child's bedside; when children sit around the campfire hearing ghostly tales; when storytellers get together for gatherings and festivals. We could imagine Listener's presence at those rare councils where the poor and the powerful hear each other's stories, or when enemies hear a note of truth in each other's voices. We could understand that Listener guides the work of scientists and researchers as well of today's storytellers. Dr. George Salt, of the University of California, used to tell his students: "Like St. Francis, zoologists must speak with animals. The trick is to speak clearly enough that the animals hear, and to listen carefully enough to make sense of their response – and never to speak so loudly that the only response was fright." For the purposes of our game, we could imagine that all of these things take place within the circle of Listener's mysterious and powerful blessing.

So here's how the game can work. Think of a moment in life or literature when someone listens to a voice that speaks from beyond the normal range of everyday perception and understanding. Find someone to tell the story to (and it must be told, not written). And at the moment when this extraordinary listening becomes possible, pretend you're telling an episode from a myth. You can even say: Listener was going along. It can't hurt, and it may work. You'll certainly feel a bit strange and self-conscious, which is appropriate given how unusual it is to pretend to be a mythteller in the early twenty-first century. Since it's just a game, and a new one at that, we're allowed to feel awkward. And, besides, we could do a lot worse in this high-tech world of ours than to imagine having a myth hero like Listener walk among us.

And now we're ready to play the game of mythtelling. The myth we're pretending we know how to tell will be a long, interconnected cycle of word of mouth, mysterious, timely, useful, memorable stories that teach us how to listen to each other, to animals, to the beyond-human realm, to rivers and galaxies, to our dreams, to our mythtelling ancestors whose voices still speak to us, and to the mouse on the fairy tale road. And as we tell these stories, these episodes of a far bigger, perhaps even world-changing story, we can imagine that Listener, the spirit at the heart of our new myth, is going along making it possible to hear the voices that could be carrying our most necessary wisdoms.

And now, I think, we can begin.

"One"

Listener was going along ….

LAST STORIES
REPORT OF THE BLUE DJINN

I'll end this logbook with two erotic yarns. "A Selkish Tale" grew out of a conversation with my storytelling friend Ron Evans, who lives just down the coast of Vancouver Island from Campbell River. He was telling me about the sea lions arriving for a big gorge on herring. "Report of the Blue Djinn" is a tribute to my beloved *Arabian Nights*, *Decameron*, and *Canterbury Tales*, which celebrate every possible form of human desire and love. If you're not in the mood for these kinds of stories, I can advise you to do what Chaucer tells his readers/listeners in the prologue to "The Miller's Tale": "Turne over the leef and chese another tale." In both stories, the sex and love being described – between and among people of different shapes and ages – gets little airplay but seems all the more worthy of celebration. A storyteller's job is to honour the stories that might otherwise be lost, untold, unheard. May both stories bring soul- and body-exhilarating joy to you when you enter the Blue Djinn's realm, alone or in the company of someone you love.

REPORT OF THE BLUE DJINN

Last night I led a Triple. Fellow djinn, I'm honoured by your invitation to report the details of this extraordinary event. I'm not boasting, but all of us know how rare it is. This was the first Triple I've produced since becoming the Blue Djinn and specializing in older lovers. Each of us has in our charge the desires and loves of our mortal cohorts. The Green Djinn is there at the first blossoming of sexual feeling. The Grey Djinn guides our oldest humans towards the gentler pleasures of hand-holding and the caresses of beloved cats. But I have the privilege of presiding over the grand flush of sensuality that is awakened and released as these mysterious, delightful creatures reach their fifties and sixties.

The Triple was awe-inspiring. My three lovers came at the same time, with three superbly uninhibited bursts of pleasure, each in their own room and by their own hand but linked inexorably by love and friendship and a mutual history of desire. I was with all of them, dancing at djinn-speed from mirror to mirror, room to room, guiding their eager hands and fingers. The two women were just dripping, hips shaking with pleasures neither had felt for a long time. The man, stiff-cocked in front of his hotel mirror, squirted long and hard and had to lie down trembling afterwards. Comrades, you will not be surprised that the sensations of their fifty-year-old bodies caused them all, at their respective moments of ecstasy, to call on the name of the One Who Made the World, the grand lyricist of human sensuality whose servants we are blessed to be.

There were many notable things to mention about last night's festival of skin, hand, and motion. One of the women, a doctor, is black, the other, a labour lawyer, is white. I say "black," but she's from one of the Islands, and her tone is more a rich coffee colour. The other woman is white – but not a pale, anemic white. She's Dutch, white like Devon cream, with gorgeous strawberry pinks in the places I'll be referring to in this report. The man, a musician, is light brown, a blend of two and a half continents' worth of immigration and cross-cultural lovemaking. They all met and loved each other, or tried to, in Montreal when they were young. They are no longer young, but they are still full of desire, and last night they were all magnificently naked, all of them pleasuring their own bodies and dreaming of each others', as they indulged in their private (well, I was there too, but we djinn aren't exactly "there") celebrations. I was cheerleading from the mirrors as their hands pulled, stroked, caressed, delicately inserted, twisted, flicked, pinched nipples and other delicious bits, and I was there to put the match to the powder when they came. It was a true Triple, for at the same moment all three, thinking about and yearning for each other, were rocked by the same great shudders, hip thrusts, and flush of flame that Worldmaker was kind enough (and mischievous enough) to hardwire into the bodies of mortal men and women. That raw, raucous body pleasure is, for djinn, a delight we can only enjoy vicariously. Shall we regret, dear comrades, or accept this destiny? Separated from certain laws of biology and physics, we must always ride shotgun as the humans revel in the exquisite pleasure systems our boss endowed them with.

So there was the man, alone in the hotel room; the doctor, in her bedroom; the lawyer in hers. They were naked, aroused in every way, aflow with desire. What were they thinking? Of past attractions, current longings, of all the men and women whose bodies they'd caressed, most of all of each other. As we djinn know best of all, sex is a gift, an offering, a joyful and abundant sacrifice to "the force that through the green fuse drives the flower," as Dylan Thomas wrote. I will do my best to report on what I beheld (bestroked, bediddled, became...) as my sweet trio joined in their djinn-linked whirl of mad pleasure.

We djinn are the spirit masters of erotic pleasure, and also its custodians. From the first awkward backseat gropings to the tender explorations of the aged, we awaken and guide and enable the wondrous excitements humans are capable of experiencing. Last night, as I raced like an electronic signal between my three lovers, aiding and abetting – and abedding! – their lovemaking, I truly saw that a body past fifty contains all of the youthful bodies its soul has inhabited since it first felt the stirring of sensual desire. My doctor, for example. She strokes her sides and runs her index finger under the top of her panties …and so she has done for many years, first as a teenager, sometimes alone, sometimes with a boyfriend, sometimes with her husbands, guiding their fingers to the places hers know so well. Her belly is fuller than it was thirty years ago, her hips wider – but the juice between her thighs, beckoned by her impatient fingers, still flowing with the same exuberance, if somewhat less plentifully, as it always has. There in her cleft her sweet volcano begins to glow when – as she's always done – she presses her lips together (her mouth and those lips lower down), teasing herself as she's always liked to do. She'll press them together in a long, smooth seal, then – much later – intrude with two or three long fingers. It's a game of Solitaire, with the highest stakes. First she'll revel in her colours, opening delicately to see in the mirror (my usual observation station) two lines of pink vulva bordered by dark brown skin, all of it surrounded by black and salt-coloured hair. She presses her lips together, then opens them with a well-placed and well-practiced fingertip. All of her former comings – so many! – are there, remembered, revealed, soon to be conjured and released.

Before I tell you more of the history that connected my three lovers, I must praise their aging bodies. Djinn, some of you may not comprehend the staggering beauty of the scene I was pleased to preside over. If you have the easier job of working with the young, the idea of three people in late middle age self-loving their respective ways into crashingly wonderful orgasms may not, for you who are accustomed to less-seasoned paramours, be appealing. But you are wrong to hold this prejudice, and, if you're ever promoted to the role of Blue Djinn, you will come to understand that there is a grace, a rhythm, a savour, an intensity of sensual delight that the young — filled with hectic hormonal forces — are not able to imagine or experience. These pleasures are reserved for those who have had years of experimentation, success, failure; who have broken hearts and had hearts broken; who have sought out solitude and joyful reunion; whose hands and minds have known hard work and heavy responsibilities. Since I've begun my service as Blue Djinn I have come to marvel at the desiring and desirability of these bodies.

My report requires a bit of history. The doctor has been married twice and has had nine lovers over the years, and one almost lover. He's the man over in the hotel. They met at McGill University, where he was studying composition and she was in medicine. It didn't go further at the time, because he was dating the other woman, who had come from Holland to Canada as an *au pair* and stayed to study. Now the musician is on tour and doing a show — he plays free jazz — in Cleveland, where the West Indian woman has been living for ten years. By chance, she saw a poster for the show, wrote him an e-mail, and arranged a post-concert get-together. They've had a lovely, friendly reunion after such a long separation (a mere moment to us djinn, but to humans, an eternity); but somehow, though they both seemed willing to shed their clothes, an old shyness held them back, and he wound up back at his hotel room, alone, fully aroused and standing in front of his hotel mirror.

The doctor's doors have all been locked, checked twice, and the lights in the kitchen downstairs left on. She lives alone and is nervous about the neighbour-hood. She's fifty-five years old. Close-up shot: She's wearing a green top, a longish skirt, and a bracelet made of milk jade and aquamarine. It glows with a restrained green light and looks stunning on her light brown wrist. She's put on a vintage calypso CD – Mighty Sparrow, I think – and has carefully shut her bedroom door. Now she sips from a glass of white wine, not too expensive but not the cheap stuff either, and she takes a few steps around the room, dancing slowly in a counter-rhythm to the jump-up beat of the carnival music.

Now she turns towards the mirror (where I'm hid-ing and guiding), reaches behind her back, and unzips her blouse. She slides it over her head and tosses it on to the bed. Before moving on to her bra, she admires her upper body in the mirror. She lifts her arms in the air and slowly turns, her hips moving slightly to the music. She undoes her bra and shakes it loose. Now her breasts sway freely, and the dark chocolate nipples harden as they emerge into the air. She lightly rakes her fingernails across her chest, right to left and back again. On the return sweep, she brushes her nipples and gives them light, quick pinches. They were already hard, but, if you're taking notes, my dear djinn, they begin to stiffen and swell and bulge and strain forward. She reaches over to a jar of cream and begins to smooth it over her breasts. The scent is sweet but tart – grapefruit? pomegranate?

Her nipples are now fully swollen, and her hands begin to slip down her sides. Mingled with the scent of the cream, she can smell the first sea salt release of sexual juices from between her legs. It is an intoxicating mixture of smells. She strokes her breasts again, then leaves them alone for a moment and slides her hands south over her stomach and then spreads them left and right until they are touching her hips. Then she presses with some vigour around the front of her thighs until her index fingers are in striking distance of her ....

I never know what to call that part of female anatomy. Believe it or not, djinn of all sensual desires, I've always been a bit shy about naming such a voluptuous fountain of pleasure. Chaucer's Wife of Bath, she of the five husbands, called it her "*belle chose*," and that will do for this report as well.

Her two index fingers stretch inward, almost touching the outer folds of her now-very-blossomed vulva, and now slowly, slowly, slowly moving towards and into her *belle chose*, which is pulsing to that calypso beat, her now-well-embedded fingers dance wildly in and around and out again and in again. The animal sound that will soon come out of her throat surprises her every time, and, if the pan band hadn't been turned up loud, it may have surprised her neighbours, too.

While all that was happening at the home of and deep within our stunning black doctor, the *Montreallaise* was taking a shower, picking up the lubricant, and walking towards the full-length mirror in her bedroom. She lives on the Plateau. A long time ago, she and the jazz musician were lovers, and they still like to see each other. What with his touring and her rather active love life, their encounters are infrequent though much-anticipated. She is a tall woman who strides more than saunters. She has a direct and unadorned manner, a straight back, broad shoulders. She is wearing a red terrycloth robe. Her hair is white, and it gleams from the shower she's just taken. She has a certain ritual. She lights a candle. She, too, puts on a CD: Dutch pop from her teenage years, and next to the player, she places a CD of an African women's choir, knowing there will be a point in the evening when, if she's not too frantic with excitement, she'll try to change the CDs to find more syncopated rhythms for her fingers and hips.

She stands in front of the mirror, then angles it so she can only see her body, not her face. This helps her imagine that her strong hands are also the hands of …well, that's where it gets interesting. The musician, who she only sees every year or two? The woman in Cleveland, who she had such a crush on so long ago? That young lawyer she met at a conference in New York two years ago and, in a thrilling moment of cannabis-aided same-sex revellry, made mad love to in a room overlooking the Palisades? In fact, as she prepares to stroke herself, she is summoning all the people who have ever caressed her exquisite curves and roundnesses.

She faces the mirror and shrugs the terrycloth robe to the floor. Unlike the doctor, who teased her breasts and pinched her nipples with such relish, our lawyer reaches into a drawer and picks out a big, dark purple vibrator. She lubricates it and spreads her legs. She giggles a little, re-membering those earnest and explicit sex education tele-vision shows that explained in detail how Dutch teenagers could masturbate, and assured them that it was Normal Behaviour for Adolescents. "Yah, and for old women, too." She grins to herself as she turns on the vibrator and slowly begins to pass it from the top to bottom of her *belle chose*. The tip of the electric rod meets her own hidden, well-oiled tip, then digs a sweet groove through her vulva to the very ass-end of her – well, I may as well say – cunt. (Such a direct approach – so Dutch – makes me want to avoid niceties and metaphors.)

The Dutch rock is pounding, and she is already riding the vibrator to a quick pre-climax. But now she stops. She turns it off. She puts it back on the shelf. She stands per-fectly still at first. Obviously, this is a woman who enjoys suspense. There are shimmers of heat coming up from her belly and rolling down her legs to her feet and toes. She begins to stroke her superbly rounded breasts, and her nipples begin to pucker with excitement. She gathers her breasts from underneath and pushes them towards the mirror, a kind of sacred offering. She touches her nipples lightly, with finesse – no sharp pinching this time. A gentle rake of nails over their hardness. A tiny shock of excitement runs over them. Then: a pinch. Then it happens.

Resistance is, as humans say, futile. Her back arches and stretches with pleasure, her stomach pulses, her *belle chose* demands the vibrator again – and when it enters, turned to its fastest rhythm, her body shudders and rocks and swoons its way to a veritable storm-gasm (I coined the term, but you're all welcome to use it in your own reports). Boom! Crash! The thunder of her vulva closing tight around the smooth, hard, fast-pulsing machine; the flashing of her blue eyes as she glances at her body in the mirror, marvelling at her own rhythms. A last thought of her horn-playing sometime paramour, then a flash of longing for the West Indian woman, then a gasp of gratitude to the goddess, then no thoughts at all as she falls backward on to the bed, still clutching the vibrator, dripping with her own juices and the ever-useful lubricant. And when it slips a little out of her sopping pussy (a common term but perhaps, in this case, the perfect nickname), she growls Dutch swear words in her deep voice, then rams it back in and has several more wild, hip-rocking explosions before she can let go.

Before I tell you what the man was doing, let me retrace the lines connecting this trio. As I mentioned, they all met in Montreal thirty years ago. The Dutch woman,

studying law at McGill, had been deeply and distract-
ingly attracted to the West Indian medical student, a
friend of the musician. It would be many years before
she allowed herself to experiment with women lovers,
and so for now she would only allow herself to gaze at
and wonder about her when they met at graduate student parties, undressing her in her imagination, pictur-
ing those dark breasts with their nut-brown nipples, the
thatch of tightly curled hair below, the sweet and amaz-
ingly danceable hips. But no advance was ever made,
and I doubt it would have gone anywhere even if she'd
had the courage to make her feelings known. (You
Green Djinn and Red Djinn, concerned as you are with
first and young loves, know of the many frustrations
and obstacles our humans experience in their earliest
desires.)

That's also when the jazz musician and doctor had
their almost fling. He had started to date the law student,
but it won't surprise any of you to know that the man
also liked and wanted to make love to his black friend.
Humans, as we know so well, are a funny species that
way. Yet he held back. His music is exuberant, expressive,
adventurous, but he is, offstage, a fairly shy man, and
even though they wanted desperately to sleep together,
he remained, as humans call it, "faithful" to his girlfriend.
This didn't prevent the two surreptitious not-quite-lovers
from taking at least some of their clothes off and becoming intimately, if briefly, acquainted with each others'
lips, breasts, and bellies. It was just enough fire to sear

them both, and they'd never forgotten how much heat had once sparked between them.

After a few years, he moved to Europe, she became an intern in Detroit and eventually settled in Cleveland, and the Dutch woman made her career in Canada. When the musician and doctor had their sweet reunion, all of the old attraction was there. All of the old shyness, too. She was single, having recently left a rather overbearing boyfriend. But, as she explained over those late-night beers, she wasn't quite ready to quit being chaste. She explained this, curiously enough, as she pressed into his arms on the sidewalk outside his hotel — then kissed him passionately, held him even harder, then told him how handsome he still was after all those years. He was thrilled, he was stunned; then, just before he could return the compliment and whisper, "Come up for a drink," her cab pulled up (she must have called it when he wasn't looking), she jumped in, and that was how they parted.

Which brings us to the man, naked and alone in his hotel room. The concert had been brilliant – a standing ovation. Now he himself has a standing "ovation" – his member erect and as hard as a sax. The warmth of his West Indian friend's body rests on his chest and hips, and he was remembering all too vividly how much he'd desired her when they were both young. He was wishing she'd come up to his hotel room but was a little bit glad she hadn't. Life was already complicated enough, he thought. He was also thinking with immense fondness of his sometimes lover in Montreal, who he hoped to see next January at the end of the tour. These imaginings have left him with a great charge of sex to offer the universe, a gift in honour of these two beautiful women.

He contemplates his body in the mirror (my favourite habitat). His stomach and chest are slim and muscular. He begins pulling his fingernails slowly across his nipples (all three seem to like such beginnings), down his flanks, around to the back, over his buttocks. A fingertip slips into the hole Worldmaker endowed with such dark, sweet, mysterious energy for both men and women. (With older humans, comrades, you will become well-acquainted with the delights of that particular constellation of erogeny.) He plays his body with the same improvisational energy he plays his music.

It is a long time before he grasps his penis, and even longer before he begins to thrust forward into his tightly interlocked hands, which rest on the edge of the table holding our mirror. No creams or lotions needed to make that handmade nest slippery; the musician's juices are so abundant, they keep beading at the top of his male member (I know – the term is clinical; should it perhaps be "*beau truc*" to match the two women's "*belles choses*"?) and flowing over on to his fingers. Sometimes a hand slips to the back of the festivities, and that teasing fingertip reawakens the small but gloriously excited hole at the bottom of his spine. He has a good voice, does our fifty-seven-year-old jazzman, and just before his cock rocks its way to its crescendo, he finds himself singing, hoarsely, an old standard: "Lace up your boots, and we'll broom on down, to a knocked-out shack at the edge of town / there's an eight-beat combo that just won't quit / keep walkin' 'til you see those blue lights lit / Fall in there, and you'll see some sights / down at the House, the House of Blue LIGHTS!!!" He comes on "lights," blasting it out through his hands, on to the table; some even splashes on the mirror. Just before collapsing backwards – and the women were coming at the same time, also panting and giving fervent praise, also with their hands wet with their own embrocations – he does a quick prayer of thanks, calling on the name of the One Who Gave Such Extravagant Gifts to those creatures who get to savour them.

And that was my – that is to say, their – rare and mighty Triple, which I was honoured to conjure and kindle and witness and bless. A rare event, to be sure, and only possible because these three had never stopped loving and desiring each other, right to the very eve of the Grey Djinn's realm.

In conclusion, O djinn, let me observe that we are not of that favoured species. We are not. We are not. We are like the electric currents connecting our human charges to Worldmaker's sublime power grid. That is our privilege, our destiny, our thrill, and, to conclude my report, our eternal regret. We spark and watch and rejoice and sanctify, but, having no bodies of our own, we can never love.

A SELKISH STORY

This isn't a selkie story, but it is a selk*ish* story. There was an inshore fisherman living just down the coastal highway from Campbell River, on the east side of Vancouver Island. He lived alone. He'd had a few relationships over the years, but nothing seemed to last, maybe because of the crazy hours he kept or or maybe just because. He loved to cook, and he loved to eat, and he was a big man, just over 300 pounds. He went up or down ten or fifteen pounds depending on the cuisines he was experimenting with. When he was on a Japanese kick, he dropped to 295. The southern Italian took him up again. He was strong, he was fit, and he was fat.

Over the years, he'd become a gourmet chef and, when he wasn't working or driving up to Campbell River or down to Nanaimo for a bit of social life, he was downloading recipes, reading cookbooks, and generally cooking up a storm. Mostly he cooked for himself, although he did take extra pies and stews down to the cluster of cabins a few hundred metres up the beach where a few indigent artists lived. Not surprisingly, he was a great connoisseur of seafood, raw and cooked.

One summer night he was out on the porch of his cabin – it wasn't far from the beach, just up a little hill – and he couldn't settle down. He'd been planning to reread Julia Child and maybe even watch the movie about her, but he felt too restless. Supper had been a lightly sautéed filet of halibut in a Reggiano crust. He'd also had a glass – well, maybe two – of west coast Zinfandel. He wasn't planning to go out the next day, so wouldn't have to get up early, but he wasn't really looking forward to a day off, either. He just felt crossways with himself and, truth be told, a little lonely. He wondered if he should call the woman he'd met from that slow food organization in Victoria who'd seemed to like him. That had been over the Net. When they actually met one day at a conference on sustainable fishing and agriculture she was less enthusiastic. He still wondered if it was because he was so big. Almost everyone else at the conference had been skinny.

From his chair on the porch, he could hear the barking of the sea lions. Everyone had gathered in the bay for the herring run: seals, sea lions, gulls, eagles. It was like a Michelin-starred aquatic bistro out there at this time of year. He walked down the path that led to the shore and stood on the beach. The moon was coming up full, and his spirits also began to lift. He stood there for a long time, sipping from his wineglass and planning dessert (there were three kinds of pie in the fridge). He listened to the surf, and to the barking of the sea lions.

Then, just before he turned to walk home, he heard a new sound. There were people laughing just around the point. Sounded like a hell of a beach party. Sometimes the teenagers would build a driftwood campfire on the beach, and he'd wander down to smoke a joint or just smile at their crazy energy. But these weren't teen voices. They were full-throated belly laughs, women by the sound of them, but all of them with unusually deep voices. He carefully placed his wineglass among the rocks, and stepped over to the point. Staying in the shadows, he peered around the boulders. To his amazement, there were about twelve or thirteen – he was too shocked to count – naked women dancing on the beach about fifty metres away! They were dancing around what looked like a pile of fur coats. They all had long brown hair, pendulous breasts that swung exuberantly as they danced, large bellies, and splendidly round bottoms. As they stamped in their circle, he could feel the beach shake a little. He wondered at first if this was a pagan ritual, maybe some local Wiccans out for a midsummer frolic. This was the west coast, after all.

But then he understood. These weren't human women. They were the seal people, the selkies he'd heard about from the old legends. But, no, in those stories the selkies were always slender and nymphlike and – at least in his fantasies – vaguely Celtic in appearance. These women were the sea *lion* people, big and brown and incredibly beautiful, dancing around their own shed skins. For creatures who waddled so gracelessly on the sand, he thought they were astonishingly fine dancers. And as they danced and shook their hair and waved their arms and undulated their bellies, they laughed and laughed under the moonlight. He wanted to laugh, too, but he stayed back in the shadows watching. It was something like a Macedonian maidens' wedding dance, except with really big, naked, brown-skinned women whom he fervently hoped weren't particularly virginal.

These women were almost as big as he was, and they were the most beautiful women he'd ever seen. Sometimes, when being alone was just too much, he'd surf the Web for pictures of naked people. He didn't do this for very long because the women on the Web never looked real. Also, he couldn't help but wonder why they were so willing to let the whole world look at them in their nakedness. He wasn't a prude, but what if their uncles, sons, or, god forbid, fathers should happen across the pictures? Still, nothing online had prepared him for these dancing women.

He felt an electric shock shoot through all 300 pounds of his big, agile body. Once, as a teenager alone in a kayak on a still, moonlit sea, he'd felt a similar tremor and thrill. That time, under the spell of a similarly full moon, he'd stripped – not easy to do in a kayak, especially for a big boy – and then come over the side, shooting silver drops of pure male life into the salt water. Now, middle-aged, the same feeling of impossibly strong desire was ramming up and down his spine. But it wasn't something to be released just like that; it was something to savour. So he watched and waited and enjoyed the show. Besides the dancers, he could see another group of sea lions swimming and floating out past the surf.

Whenever he'd heard the old stories, he'd always wondered what *he'd* do if he came upon a bunch of selkies boogying on a beach. Would he steal a skin and force the prettiest one to live with him like they always did in the legends? He hadn't thought he would because a) it just seemed wrong, and b) he thought it wouldn't be much fun for someone that different to live among his people. He just couldn't imagine her shopping at the Walmart in Campbell River. But now, watching the sea lion women dance, he couldn't help himself.

He came around the rocks, keeping to the shadows. He waited until the dancers moved away from the pile of skins, and then tiptoed forward, picked up a skin, and hustled away with it up the beach. It was heavy! As strong as he was, it took all his strength to pack it back around the point. He tucked it away in a crevice and then peered back around the boulders.

All of the women had put on their sea lion skins and were waddling back toward the water. But there was one still standing there, looking around. She wasn't laughing anymore. In fact, she made a strangely delicate growling sound that he understood was a kind of cry. The others had now dived into the surf and were watching their sister standing there alone. He looked at her, too. She was magnificently naked, her breasts so full and voluptuous, her belly a great, soft swelling, her back curving into two thrillingly round shapes. The fisherman was thunderstruck with both the quality *and* quantity of her loveliness.

He had never felt such desire in his life.

He must have kicked a pebble on the shale, because she looked over. The moon was so bright he could see a tear standing in the corner of one of her warm, brown eyes.

The fisherman didn't think twice. He turned back to the supple, bulky skin, pulled it carefully from his hiding place, and ran as fast as he could toward the sea lion woman. Legend be damned, he thought, this belongs to her! Hauling it down the beach, and weeping as he walked, he laid it carefully at her feet. He averted his eyes, from shame at what he'd tried to do, and from sheer horniness. He put it down and turned to flee – and then stopped, because he felt her hand on his arm. She delicately turned him around to face her. Then she slid her hand down so she could interlace her fingers with his. With her other hand she brushed away the tears – of love? of frustration? of a lifetime of loneliness? of hope? – that shone in his eyes. She leaned towards him, opened his shirt, and smelled his chest. It must have pleased her because she let out a kind of guttural murmur of what he hoped was her sound for desire. Then she licked him, not once but many times all around his muscular breasts. He could smell her hair. It smelled a lot like halibut. He decided that it worked for him. Yes, she smelled like a sea creature, but he was, indeed, an aficionado. Plus he could start to smell the other intoxicating odours that came up from her lower body.

He overcame his bachelor shyness and touched her tear away, too. And then the woman opened her great arms to him and hugged him. She was strong! She was massive! So was he! At first he tensed up, but it didn't take long before he began to shake and tremble from desire, and then he took her in his arms, and began to relax and relax and relax, and then – finally – to smile with an idiot joy. If he'd had any drinking buddies, what a yarn he'd be able to spin over a few beers. But he didn't, and this wasn't the kind of thing his recipe listserv companions would be interested in reading. No, this adventure would only be for himself and her.

He let his arms slide down her smooth back. They came to rest on the sweet, impressive outswellings below. She sighed and panted. A smell of kelp and sex surrounded them. Then she stepped away from him, and, for one heartbreaking moment, he thought she was going to grab her skin and run back to the sea. But instead she knelt on the sand and spread the sea lion skin to make a blanket, and then lay down on it and looked up at him with a smile. He looked and looked, feasting his eyes on the long hair spread out around her, at her breasts that rose and balanced on either side with exhilarating abandon.

Then, moving very slowly, utterly flushed with desire, the fisherman knelt between her legs and reached out to her surprisingly up-pointing nipples. Her legs were almost as big as his. Where her thighs met, he saw a great patch of brown hair, rough and spreading. She smiled up at him and then laughed that full-throated laugh of her people in their human form. He quickly threw his clothes off and sank on to the softness of her breasts, her belly, her thighs. She was ready to take him in, and there, on the beach, under the moonlight, our BC fisherman and his sea lion paramour made love. They made love, they *made* love, and love *made* them. They were alone, except for a group of brown-eyed heads watching from just past the breakers. It was quiet, except for the barking of the sea lions, who seemed to time their crescendi to the cadence of the lovers' rocking, rollicking hips.

And then everything became much more urgent: the sea, the surf, the moon, the woman enfolding his big body with hers, the barking of her companions. Then both of them made sounds they'd never made before. He surprised himself by giving out a great, almost-barking cry of joy, and she yelled out with an almost-operatic high C. When he could speak a human language again, all he could murmur was, "Godgodgodgod .... thankyouthankyouthankyou...." And she spoke, too, something between a human and a sea lion tongue, and it sounded to his ears like she used the sweetest series of vowels he'd ever heard, perhaps invoking whatever deity sea lions call upon when they come.

She kissed him again and again, but more and more

gently, until he fell asleep.

He woke up at dawn. He was lying on the sand, and a shelter of driftwood arched over him. The beach was empty, the sea was calm. He sat for a long time listening to the surf. Then he began to laugh and cry at the same time. When he finished, he found his clothes, dressed, and slowly walked back up the path to home.

It was a good season for fishing that year. It was also a good season for cooking. He submitted a recipe to a seafood contest in Victoria, and won. He met someone there who shared his passion for cooking and baking and eating. She ended up moving up the coast, and they lived together for many years. Sometimes, on moonlit nights in the summer, they'd take a blanket and a bottle of excellent west coast wine and maybe a pie or two down to the beach. Sometimes they'd stay there all night, dozing off to the sound of the surf. Sometimes, just before kissing her full, round belly, he'd glimpse a sea lion bobbing out past the breakers, watching him and his big, lovely, human wife make love. He'd smile to himself, remembering.